Fiction and Society

Fiction and Society

Narrativisation of Realities in the Novels of Shashi Deshpande and Githa Hariharan

Sarita Prabhakar

RAWAT PUBLICATIONS
Jaipur • New Delhi • Bangalore • Hyderabad • Guwahati

ISBN 978-81-316-0387-1

Published by
Prem Rawat for **Rawat Publications**
Satyam Apts, Sector 3, Jawahar Nagar, Jaipur 302 004 (India)
Phone: 0141 265 1748 / 7006 Fax: 0141 265 1748
E-mail: info@rawatbooks.com
Website: www.rawatbooks.com

New Delhi Office
4858/24, Ansari Road, Daryaganj, New Delhi 110 002
Phone: 011 2326 3290

Also at *Bangalore, Hyderabad* and *Guwahati*

Typeset by Rawat Computers, Jaipur
Printed at Chaman Enterprises, New Delhi

Contents

Preface

The idea of looking at women writers as writers and not as 'women' writers was something that inspired me to take up the works of Shashi Deshpande and Githa Hariharan, the two contemporary Indian writers writing in English who constitute a pluralistic world wherein the Indian heritage, the indigenous forms, the inherited and internalised cultural values, the oral tradition all jostle with each other. Their works also argue for the continuance and existence of a distinct oral tradition in Indian culture and refuse to talk of an Indian tradition in singular when Indianness itself defies categorisation by virtue of its heterogeneity and diversity. The work while not denying the role of gender, explores the narrative style of two writers, reading their works closely to see how they use stories and the impact these stories have on the structure of their works. The work also aims at locating these two writers, who have used oral and written versions of the *Panchtantra;* the *Ramayana* and the *Mahabharata;* the storytelling traditions and techniques, in the multiple contexts of the present and the multiple traditions of the past. The study works through a socio-cultural approach tracing the connectivity between the past and the present, between tradition and contemporary society as both the writers go on to rewrite the past through their focus on myths, fables, social reforms and *Upanishads* and also works towards relating the tradition of the oral narratives, grandmother's tales, interaction between members in the household.

The study has been divided into seven chapters. The opening chapter gives a glimpse into the contemporary literary scene as well as into the contemporary critical idiom and the stance these two writers have adopted. It also raises several questions related to the act of storytelling which have been answered in the subsequent chapters and also includes a critical survey of the works already available on these writers. The second, third, and the fourth chapters, focusing on the mythological stories, real-life stories and the stories of survival embedded in the works of these two writers, show the writers' politics at work and that the politics is worked out in terms of the relationship between characters themselves and between characters and their environment through the deployment of diverse narratives. These narratives can be mythological or real. The fifth chapter explores the nature of storytelling, the role of memory in it and its relation to truth. It also looks at the self reflexivity inherent in their narratives. The sixth chapter shows how these embedded stories then are not just additional to the narratives but are important and integral both in terms of a form and content. The final chapter is in the form of a conclusion.

The work is based on my doctoral research and I have incurred several debts during this research. First of all, I express my gratitude to my supervisor Professor Veena Singh for her constant support and guidance in accomplishing this work. I am grateful to my friends and co-researchers and above all my revered teacher Professor Jasbir Jain who has always been a source of inspiration for me. My thanks are due to my father Dr. Manohar Prabhakar, my husband Anil Gupta and my sons Ayush and Apoorv for their loving support.

I also owe a great deal to the Department of English, University of Rajasthan for its co-operation at all stages of my work. My thanks are also due to Central Library, Jaipur, the Sahitya Akademi and the British Council Library, Delhi for rendering all possible help in making the latest books, magazines and journals available.

Sarita Prabhakar

CHAPTER 1

Introduction

> No text is original, yet no telling is a mere retelling—and the story has no closure, although it may be enclosed in a text ... the stories are there, 'always already'.
>
> — **A.K. Ramanujan** (2004: 158)

People in all times and places have told stories. In fact story-telling is a basic form of communication, both natural and universal. Reynolds Price in his introduction to *A Palpable God* describes the intrinsic nature of stories when he writes:

> A need to tell and hear stories is essential to the species Homo sapiens-second in necessity apparently after nourishment and before love and shelter. Millions survive without love or home, almost none in silence; the opposite of silence leads quickly to narrative, and the sound of story is the dominant sound of our

> lives, from the small accounts of our days' events to the vast incommunicable constructs of psychopaths. (1978: 3)

All stories, from the simple to the complex one, arise out of some need of human beings and are frequently used to teach, explain, and/or to entertain as well as for a host of other purposes. It is through storytelling that we assess and interpret events, share our experiences and pass on accumulated wisdom; beliefs and values. Stories also connect us with past, present and future by teaching us to anticipate the possible consequences of our actions. Stories, thus, have been playing an important role in the complex process of human development right from the beginning of human civilisation. The earliest form of storytelling has been primarily oral. It is through the oral tradition that cultures of different societies have been preserved and the experiences, morals, histories of the older generations have been passed to the younger ones. With the invention of writing and the use of media, stories were recorded, transcribed and shared over wide regions of the world. This, however, does not imply that storytelling is a thing of the past. Storytelling and story listening are the basic ways of thinking about the world and continue to play their role in our lives at multifarious levels.

Though basic and intrinsic, the act of storytelling is in itself a complex one. By its very nature, it implies a teller and a listener. What is the role of a teller in a story? Is it a simple, naïve act of narration or does one's perspective and perception affect this act of narrating events? If so then, can two tellings of the same story be exactly alike? Is there a shift in the perspective when the same story is narrated by a person of different gender? Does this affect the subject matter also? What is the role of the listener? Does he passively 'receive' the story?

Storytelling is obviously a phenomenon of the oral tradition; the novel a product of literacy. Then, why is storytelling being used widely in fiction as a technique and structural principle? Why the framework of story-within-a story is used? Are the embedded stories redundancies or variations which form an integral part of the narrative structure?

The digressional method of storytelling is perhaps the oldest device used in the Indian classical texts such as the *Ramayana,* the *Mahabharata* and the *Panchtantra* which are written but technically part of the oral tradition. Fluidity is an essential characteristic of the oral tradition. No two tellings of a story can be exactly the same. There are a number of versions available of the legend of Rama, Sita, Lakshamana and Ravana throughout the country as well as outside it. A.K. Ramanujan in "Three Hundred Ramayanas: Five Examples and Three Thoughts on Translation", pointing to the various versions of the *Ramayana,* writes: "How many Ramanayas? Three hundred? Three thousand?" (2004: 131). He further shows how these hundreds of telling of a story in different cultures, languages and religious traditions get 'translated', 'transplanted' and 'transported'. This malleability in the very nature of telling a story has attracted a number of writers and is being widely used as a technique and structural principle.

In fact, the twentieth century fiction, on the whole, evinces a radical and significant departure from the fiction of the earlier period, more so in its use of form and technique. This, however, does not imply that the writers of the earlier period neglected matters of form and narrative technique, but the realistic/mimetic tradition being dominant in most writing about the novel, these were considered basically as means of representing reality. The novel was characterised by a strong interest in plot and was often marked strongly by the authorial presence and intrusiveness. The author was the 'intrusive narrator', who frequently commented on his characters, evaluating their actions and motives, expressing his views about human life in general, all to be taken as authoritative. Moral instructions from a dominant authorial position also formed a great deal of writing. Twentieth century literature, literary criticism and literary theory have posed a challenge to the idea of realism and authority. Nietzsche, who is often regarded as the father or forerunner of postmodernism, stressed that the language through which we express our knowledge is a self-contained world, entirely separate from external reality and so what we think of as knowledge is a human creation or artistic construct. A number of French thinkers were attracted to the ideas of Nietzsche. Of these, Michel Foucault and Jacques Derrida were the most significant for the development of postmodernism. Derrida asserted that there is 'nothing outside the text' as there is no correspondence between language and fact, between words and things. Within language there is a whole range of discourse and so what we call reality is itself a form of discourse that we construct. Michel Foucault saw power as the determinant of truth and knowledge and therefore objectivity as a myth. He saw the structures of power embedded in particular forms of language use and institutional practices, which dictate how the individual would perceive his world and conceptualise it. Despite significant differences among these thinkers, they all stressed the subjective and relative nature of reality. Henry James in "The Art of Fiction" reassesses the nature of the novel in the light of such relativism:

> It goes without saying that you will not write a good novel unless you possess the sense of reality; but it will be difficult to give you a recipe for calling that sense into being. Humanity is immense and reality has a myriad forms … . It is equally excellent and inconclusive to say that one must write from experience … . What kind of experience is intended, and where does it begin and end? Experience is never limited and it is never complete; it is an immense sensibility, a kind of huge spider-web, of the finest silken threads, suspended in the

> chamber of consciousness and catching every air-borne particle in its tissue. It is the very atmosphere of the mind; and when the mind is imaginative—much more when it happens to be that of a man of genius—it takes to itself the faintest hints of life, it converts the very pulses of the air into revelations. (1962: 26)

What Henry James is emphasising here is the fluid and complex nature of reality which cannot be comprehended and projected in its totality and so even when a writer engages himself with reality, it is his personal comprehension of reality born out of the myriad impressions that he receives. Therefore, reality, according to him, is not a static figuration but a version of one's own individualised perception. Bakhtin, one of the most important twentieth century theorists of the novel, also stressed the idea that 'reality as we have it ... is only of many possible realities'. Emphasising the autonomy of the novel, he saw it as a process and not as an end and therefore inconclusive, open-ended and better qualified to represent reality. While examining Dostoevsky's poetics, he brought in some of the key concepts—heteroglossia, carnival and dialogism, i.e., novels with multiple points of view, multiple meanings and multiple voices which are the characteristics of most of the novels today. Raymond Williams in "Realism and Contemporary Novel" dwells upon the rise of a new form of realist tradition which is not a discontinuation of the realist tradition, but rather an extension of the earlier realist tradition. To quote him:

> The old, naive realism is in any case dead, for it depended on a theory of natural seeing which is now impossible. When we thought we had only to open only our eyes to see a common world, we could suppose that realism was a simple recording process from which any deviation was voluntary. We now know that we literally create the world we see and that this human creation—a discovery of how we can live in the material

> world we inhabit is necessarily dynamic and active, the old static realism of the passive observer is merely a hardened convention. (1972: 590)

Modern realism, as Ian Watt has pointed out, "... begins from the position that truth can be discovered by the individual through his senses" (12: 1959). The key word here is individual.

Contemporary fiction does reflect the realities of the society, rather in many ways elements of ordinary everyday experience are more visible in it than before. It is merely that today reality is conceived differently as a result of which the traditional novel with a clear vision and a neat structure has begun to lose its appeal to the contemporary writers. The writer questions the very basis of any certainty and challenges the concept of reality and truth not to deny them, but to interrogate them in relation to experience and works within the framework of multiplicity, heterogeneity, plurality, rather than binary opposition and exclusion. Jasbir Jain in her book *Beyond Postcolonialism* elaborates upon the shift in concerns, themes and techniques in India after the forties:

> The post-1947 novel in India works with multiplicities: multiple languages, multi-subjectivities, themes and discourses, multiple memories, perspectives and landscapes. It resists any definition in the singular and moves freely between oral traditions and modernist-postmodernist experiments ... . The concern with the glorification of the ascetic figure, whether of man or woman, which engaged the writing of our earlier writers like Hari Narayan Apte in *Mein*, Tagore in *Gora* and other Gandhian portrayals has now moved into the background. The need to explain one's culture to the outsider is no longer dominant. Instead the writer is interested in exploring it for herself, in entering into a dialogue with contemporary reality, in articulating the hitherto unsaid or unheard ... . This has given birth to a new realism ... . (2006: 12–13)

Pre-independence period was preoccupied with Gandhian ideology, freedom struggle, oppression by the coloniser and resistance against it. It worked within a framework of binary opposition. After that writers sought to define protest and dissent in more specific and individual terms. In the writings of Nayantara Sehgal, Manohar Malgonkar and several other writers writing in other Indian languages, there is no extensive reference to historical events in the conventional sense, rather the aftermath of the Partition is described in terms of the psychological and emotional impact. Description is replaced by interrogation and introspection.

Twentieth century experiments have been characterised by varying of almost all the features that marked early fictional writings. There are novels almost without plot such as Bama's *Sangati: The Events*; novels in verse such as Vikram Seth's *The Golden Gate*, works of non-fiction such as Suketu Mehta's *Maximum City: Bombay Lost and Found*, novels of magic realism such as Salman Rushdie's *Midnight's Children* or Githa Hariharan's *When Dreams Travel*. At times there is a breakdown of form or a combination of different forms as in the works of writers like Rohinton Mistry, Shashi Deshpande, Githa Hariharan, Gita Mehta and Salman Rushdie where there is the straddling of the two traditions of storytelling and novel writing. There is no conventional beginning, middle or end. There are no finished characters, no finished plots. The author does not offer solutions as often there is no solution. All that he does is that he creates alternative possibilities. There is no authorial omniscience and intrusiveness. Even when a writer uses omniscient mode of narration, it is not authoritative. The narrator is in some way subject to ironic scrutiny which creates an ironic gap between his understanding of the real which is limited and the idea of an objective reality which itself is a suspect.

Freud has also had enormous effect on modern literature as a result of which detailed external description of things has been replaced by the psychological study of the states of consciousness. Virginia Woolf in "Modern Fiction" asserts that life is not as simple and systematic as it appears to be and that inner life is bafflingly complex. Interpreting it at length, she writes:

> Life is not a series of gig lamps symmetrically arranged; life is a luminous halo, a semi-transparent envelope surrounding us from the beginning of consciousness to the end. Is it not the task of the novelist to convey this varying, this unknown and uncircumscribed spirit, whatever aberration or complexity it may display, with as little mixture of the alien and external as possible? (1972: 88–89)

Today, no writer can do away with the memory and the subconscious. A number of writers have used dreams, fantasies and chains of association as structural devices. Time is also a major preoccupation with the writers of the twentieth century. Henri Bergson, the French philosopher distinguished between 'scientific time' and 'real duration' and claimed that the former is essentially an illusion, it is our subjective experience of time which is 'real'. Writers today are primarily concerned with what Bergson termed as 'real duration' and deal with time in terms of individual human experience. The narrative moves freely between present and past. The reader has to adjust continually to the different time frames. Flashback technique is also being used widely. Through flashback, the author can not only bring in the past whenever it is most relevant to the present, but also probe the past in terms of the present. Since this technique works through memory, which is by its very nature subjective and unstable, it also helps the writer to explore reality in its multiplicity and is thus organic to the new approach to reality.

A number of writers have subscribed to a cyclical version of time. In India, this notion comes from its own metaphysical framework where the divisibility of time into its units is seen only as a worldly manifestation of permanent or real time. In several Indian languages the word for yesterday and tomorrow is the same obliterating the difference between past and future. As Sudhir Kakar points out, "The words denoting time itself are given much more cavalier treatment. The word 'Kal' derived from 'Kala' can mean tomorrow or yesterday, a moment or an age, it may refer to an event which just happened, or to a future likelihood" (2002: 46). This cyclical version of time has led to a questioning of history as a monolithic structure and a linear progression of events. E.H. Carr in *What is History* defines history as "a continuous process of interactions between the historian and his facts, an unending dialogue between the present and the past" (1961: 30).

In fact, postmodernist analysis of representation and narrative and the implications of post-linguist theories as expounded by Barthes and Derrida have affected history more than any other discipline. Recent years have witnessed a number of scrutinising questions and issues being raised on the nature and character of history and its claims to truth. By highlighting the ways historians select events, and recreate them through the medium of language, the postmodernists underline the 'constructed' nature of it. Keith Jenkins writes:

> History ... Is constructed by present-minded, ideologically positioned workers ... . That past appropriated by historians is never the past itself, but a past evidenced by its remaining and accessible traces and transformed into historiography through a series of theoretically and methodically disparate procedures ... . Understood in this way, as a rhetorical, metaphorical textual practice governed by distinctive but never homogeneous procedures through which the maintenance/transformation of the past is regulated ... historical construction can be seen as taking place entirely in the present ... . In this way histories are fabricated without 'real' foundations beyond the textual ... . (1995: 178–9)

Levi-Strauss in *The Savage Mind* questions: "a historical fact is what really took place, but where did anything take place? Each episode in a revolution or war resolves into a multiple of individual psychological movements" (1996: 257). History therefore, he argues, is a matter of selection and point of view. Not only this, selection on the part of the historian involves erasure also which may result in falsification. Emphasising this point, Shashi Deshpande writes in *A Matter of Time*:

> Historians, even the most brilliant of them, are like magicians. With flamboyance they draw your attention to what they want you to see, take away from it what they want to conceal. 'Look!' they will say, 'the Queen of Spades'. And you see 'the Queen of Spades' All else is concealed in the darkness of a deliberate deceit. ... Yes that is how it is. Only God, or whoever it is standing outside the game, can see whole of it. (98–99)

The understanding that history cannot be written objectively and that there can be no absolute interpretation or final word about any event has made it possible to ask many a questions which were never asked before and has thereby assisted in reshaping our understanding of the past. The postmodern novel has played a vital role in the general movement as it has often called into question the dividing line between fact and fiction.

The blending of myth and history is a widespread form used in postmodernist fiction which is a part of narrative strategy. Emphasising the fictionality of the fiction through the use of myth and the claim of the text on reality through history, the writer renders critical the obvious distinction between fact and fiction. Such texts are both interpretative and investigative. The author revisits the past, not to glorify it or to reject it in a desire to construct an entirely new identity, but to find answers to the problems in the present. The past is retained and incorporated by means of reinterpretation, deconstruction or dilution or by way of discriminating inclusion or exclusion so as to make it more relevant in the present. Salman Rushdie's *Midnight's Children* entwines the various events in the life of the central character Saleem with the political history of India and Pakistan and explores the gap between what seems real and experiential reality. The narrative does not slip into a record of events in chronological order, rather attempts have been directed towards understanding individual life in terms of historical forces as well as the complex socio-political realities of India. The line between the past and the present, between different periods of time is erased: "Time, in my [Saleem] experience, has been ... variable and inconstant ... no people whose word for "yesterday" is the same as their word for 'tomorrow' can be said to have a firm grip on time" (1981: 106). The novel, in the words of Stephen Slemon, "destabilises history's fixity, its givenness and opens it up to the transformative power of imaginative revision" (1988: 159). It subverts the 'conventions of realism' without abandoning reality.

In Shashi Tharoor's *The Great Indian Novel* we find an interweaving of the main events of twentieth century Indian political history with those of the events, episodes and characters from the *Mahabharata*. There are some striking parallels. The episode of the disrobing of Draupadi has been used as a parallel for the 'dushasan' that prevailed in India when Indira Gandhi declared emergency. But the novel does not make simple comparisons. There is a dismantling of both myth and history which is achieved through the playful use of parody, irony, self referentiality and indeterminacy. The story is narrated by Ved Vyas to Gandpathi who comments upon the seminal nature of stories: "Have I, you seem to be asking, come to the end of my story? How forgetful you are: it was just the other day I told you stories never end, they just continue somewhere else. In the hills and the plains, the hearths and hearts, of India" (418). The idea of an objective reality is also subverted. Ved Vyas wonders in the novel: "How much one may select, interpret and arrange the living past before truth is jeopardised by inaccuracy?" Then he recommends: "No more certitudes ... . Accept doubt and diversity .... Admit there is more than one Truth, more than one Right, more than one dharma." (418). Continuities between past, present and future are established. Vyasa tells Ganapathi: "we are all living in an eternal present in which what was and what will be is contained in what is" (163). In the end Ved Vyasa tells Ganapathi: "Let us begin again" and the novel ends with the sentence with which it began establishing the circularity of time. The cyclical version of time in both the novels has enabled the writers to view events in their totality.

It is against this backdrop that I have made an attempt to evaluate the works of Shashi Deshpande and Githa Hariharan, who are exploring the possibilities of coming to terms with the past in multiple ways, even when they are, to quote Josna E. Rege, "neither shoring up a disintegrating discourse of nation nor making dramatic departure from women's traditional conflicts and concerns" (2003: 204).Where do these two writers stand in the contemporary literary scene? Can they be best described as writers belonging to the school of realism, or do they defy the traditional categorisation of writing the 'realist' novels? What is the role of storytelling and embedded stories in their novels? Are these stories mere surface narration of events, or are they doing something more and if so how have they affected the narrative structure? An attempt has been made to answer these queries in the following chapters.

Shashi Deshpande was born in the year 1938 in Dharwad. She is the daughter of the renowned dramatist and Sanskrit scholar, Shriranga. At the age of fifteen she went to Bombay, graduated in Economics and then moved to Bangalore where she got a degree in Law. She also took a course in journalism and for a short time worked with a magazine. Her writing career began in the 1970s. She has so far written ten novels and several volumes of short stories. *Roots and Shadows* was awarded the Thirumati Rangammal Prize for the best Indian novel of 1982–83 and *That Long Silence* was awarded the Sahitya Akademi Award in 1991. *The Dark Holds No Terrors* has been translated into German and Russian. She has experimented with the genre of the detective novel and also has written for children. In addition, there is a collection of essays titled *Writing from the Margin* in which she makes several significant statements about the feminist positions, fictional form and experiments. The past and the extent to which individuals are determined by forces contained within it, form a continual theme in her novels leading to a vigorous analysis of the institution of family and marriage. Though there is a recurrence of certain themes, yet with every novel she explores new areas of human psyche and human relationships. Her later novels, *Small Remedies* and *A Matter of Time*, are more concerned with the human condition than just the female psyche and condition. There is an interlacing of myths in almost all her works. The idea of the self as a complex, fluid being remains central to her work. This is brought out very vividly in the novel *Moving On* where she writes:

> ... we humans are the greatest marvels in creation; we are also the greatest mysteries to ourselves. I continue to be amazed by the genius, the questioning nature, the ceaseless probing of humans to resolve the mysteries of the universe, the way in which, gradually but surely, so many mysteries have been resolved. Yet, the enigma of our own selves remains unfathomable. The ego, the libido, the unconscious—how little they explain! Such tiny dots on a vast uncharted map. The truth is that each one of us is a universe more complicated than the limitless universe we inhabit. (111)

Deshpande's latest novel *is In the Country of Deceit* which has come out in the year 2009. Githa Hariharan, a younger writer (b.1954), was born in Coimbatore. She grew up in Bombay and Manila. From there she moved to the USA, where she continued her studies and also worked for television channels. Returning to India in 1979, she worked in Mumbai, Chennai and New Delhi, initially as an editor in a publishing house, and later as a freelancer. Presently, she lives in Delhi. She has published five novels and two volumes of short stories. She has also edited a volume of short stories in English translated from four South Indian languages called *A Southern Harvest* and has co-edited a collection of stories for children. Her work has been translated into French, Spanish, Italian, Dutch, Greek, Urdu and Malayalam. Her essays and fiction have also been included in several collections and anthologies such as Salman Rushdie's *Mirror Work: 50 Years of Indian Writing*. Hariharan reworks ancient myths, legends, folktales both from the east and the west and makes them a vehicle of new vision. Her first novel *The Thousand Faces of Night*, which won the Commonwealth Writer Prize for the best first novel in the Eurasian region, is a reworking of myths from the *Ramayana* and *Mahabharata*. The novel explores the gaps found in these myths and subverts the traditional interpretations. In her next novel *The Ghosts of Vasu Master*, once again, she subverts the conventional pattern of education with the help of fables. *When Dreams Travel* is a retelling of the stories of *The Arabian Nights* and framed by fantasy and magic realism. The novel explores power politics in relation to gender. Over the years, Hariharan has come to inhabit a very distinct space, those of the creative writers responding to political events which she makes no attempt to allegorise. Rather, they are present in all their starkness, irony and tragedy. In *In Times of Siege*, she takes up the most burning problem—the rise of fundamentalism. Her most recent novel *Fugitive Histories* can be said to be in continuum with *In Times of Siege*. In her collection of short stories *The Art of Dying*, she deals with those aspects of women's lives that have been erased, ignored, or mystified. The stories explore the concepts of 'decency' and 'honour' with playful irony. *The Winning Team* is a collection of short stories for children.

One may naturally enquire as to why these two writers have been bracketed together. Apart from the fact that both are contemporary living writers, they share certain things. The portrayal of the individual within a complex web of human relationships by means of a diversity of narratives, forms a major part of their fictional vision. Reconstruction of the past with a view to make it more meaningful for the present is also their major concern. Both of them have employed the form of a story within a story what Borges calls 'a labyrinthine quality'. They present a subject, dissect it and link it with other related themes and then put them together in a complicated mosaic. Weaving in stories within stories is an oral form of narration used in Indian classical texts such as the *Kathasaritsagar*, the *Buddhist Jataka Tales* and the *Panchtantra*. The appearance of any new character necessitates inserting a new story within the previous one-a process which Tzvetan Todorov in his analysis of the narrative technique of the *Thousand and One Nights*, labels as 'enchassement' (embedding). In the *Mahabharata* also, there are stories within stories, innumerable legends, episodes and the main story serves as a link which holds them together. Sometimes the main story seems almost forgotten or lost, but then it is taken up again which makes the narrative move on to the level of flux. There is no linear development. The core of the story remains intact but it goes on adding, multiplying and expanding its body aiming to see life in its totality. The straddling of the two traditions of storytelling and novel-writing in Shashi Deshpande and Githa Hariharan has made their task quite challenging The plot in their works is not a premeditated structure imposed upon the events, rather it grows naturally out of the character and the initial incident. Both of them believe that writing is a process of discoveries, 'a groping into the dark'. People are both complex and complicated and hence they cannot be defined and delineated in one way or in any fixed manner. In an interview given to Anuradha Marwah, Githa Hariharan says:

> I am not interested in a "photographic" view of relationships. I am anxious to go well beyond the banal or the obvious, to allow for contradictions and ambiguity in every relationship, whether it is between a man and a woman, or two women, or indeed, the relationship between a person and her dreams and desires. (*Pioneer*, February 7, 1999)

Similarly, Shashi Deshpande in "Writing and Activism" says:

> People are both complex and complicated, and therefore writing, good writing that is, ultimately provides a complex and complicated picture, not the simple picture that would emerge if the writer were writing with the intent of speaking against social evils or for social reform .... The writer explores the gaps, the silences, the ambiguities, the complexities, the contradictions-and this, not to get to any kind of a conclusion, because often there is no conclusion. (2005: 25–29)

Both writers are keenly interested in their craft and feel that one has to be a writer first and an activist later. In "Discreet Thoughts" Githa Hariharan writes:

> For some reason all of us like to imagine that a writer is a writer because he has a great deal to say (message) or is a good egg (social concern). Both these should be there, but really, in the ultimate analysis, a writer is a writer because she has a narrative skill—a balancing act she can perform. (2004: 214)

The fictional works of both the writers remind us that the relationship between traditions of committed social realism and that of the postmodernist tradition of experimentation can be a seamless one, stretching the traditional elements of representation to perturb and not to rupture its mimetic nature. Whereas the fragmented interior monologues on the part of the protagonists are an evidence of the modernist strain on the process of representation, storytelling, which constitutes a very significant part of the narrative structure, is convergent of the pre-modernist and the postmodernist techniques. They go on to explore the nature of storytelling and its relation to truth. Intertextuality, born out of their vast store of reading, also constitutes one of the major structural devices.

In many of their interviews and essays, Shashi Deshpande and Githa Hariharan have commented upon the various aspects of their own writing and the stance they have adopted. Both find the mainstream theory of literature 'abhorrent'. According to them, all writing that probes with honesty and artistry into the human situation is mainstream literature. They continue to write their own kind of fiction with rare insights, but they often feel a sense of alienation. In her essay "Where Do We Belong" included in *Writing from the Margin and Other Essays*, Shashi Deshpande feels unhappy about the increasing number of divides: 'a kind of caste system being created among the writers—regional languages pitted against English, English writers living in India against writers living abroad, diasporic writers against rooted writing etc.', and wonders where she belongs (2003: 51). She also objects to the idea of being called 'a third world writer' or 'a post colonial writer' as these labels not only limit one's writing, but also because they put one in a slot making him or her 'the other' (2003: 53). In her conversation with Arnab Chakladar, Githa Hariharan also expresses her anger over being pushed into corners. Though both of them agree that their work is influenced in some way or the other by feminism, both are equally uncomfortable being categorised as 'women writers', for there are several other things in their writing which are missed out as a result of this kind of categorisation. In her conversation with Gita Viswanath, Shashi Deshpande says:

> I do not write as a feminist novelist. But my ideology is going to permeate my writing; my feeling, thoughts and ideas about women are very important parts of my ideology. But I have other agendas also. By agendas I do not mean I set out to write with a specific agenda. There are other things that do matter to me and that do come into my writing. I mean human relationships, not just women but what human beings in general are like—these are equally important parts of my writing and when I am called a feminist writer, these are missed out and this is what I really object to. (2005: 228)

In her conversation with Arnab Chakladar, Githa Hariharan also says:

> Being a writer and a feminist doesn't mean you write tracts … . But I didn't/don't have a blueprint. As for being a "woman writer" I would say such a label is legitimate or useful only if it is used with some rigor. It is useful to study women's writing and Dalit writing and so on in an academic context. I don't think it is terribly useful if the labels become lazy, a way to ghettoize. (online version)

Both Shashi Deshpande and Githa Hariharan have attracted critical attention but most of the critics have focused on their women protagonists and issues related to feminist concerns. The first full-length work on Shashi Deshpande was brought out by Sarabjit Sandhu in 1991 titled *The Image of Woman in the Novels of Shashi Deshpande*. The work is a study of the images women are fitted into but it does not probe into the processes that go into the making of those images. The second full-length study by

Vinay Kirpal and Mukt Atrey titled *Shashi Deshpande: A Feminist Study of her Fiction* (1998) also works within the feminist framework, concentrating on the self-image of the protagonists, their constructions of the self and issues related to tradition and modernity. Mrinalini Sebastian's *The Novels of Shashi Deshpande in Postcolonial Arguments* (2000) is a departure from these two works. Destabilising the tendency to label certain novels as postcolonial on the mere basis of content, it raises several questions like what makes authors eligible to be termed postcolonial and what happens when a postcolonial critic is confronted by a seemingly apolitical novel. One of the shortcomings of the work is that focusing on Bhabha, Spivak and Said, it devotes more pages to postcolonial arguments than to Deshpande. Still the work is valuable as it poses a number of questions. Perhaps the most comprehensive work done on Shashi Deshpande is by Jasbir Jain in *Gendered Realities, Human Spaces: the Writing of Shashi Deshpande* (2003). Beginning with a close analysis of Shashi Deshpande's novels as well as her short stories, the work looks at psychological inputs, her use of myths, the narrative strategies she employs, and her native concerns. *Shashi Deshpande* by Amrita Bhalla (2006) also goes beyond the parameters of labels and descriptions and locates and places the works of Shashi Deshpande in the context of Indian society of which she writes.

There are several other edited volumes which contain essays solely on Deshpande by different scholars. In *The Fiction of Shashi Deshpande* edited by R.S. Pathak (1998), though there are a few essays which explore other aspects, the volume works mainly through feminist approach. A far better critical evaluation is available in *Writing Difference: The Novels of Shashi Deshpande* (2005) edited by Chanchala K Naik. The volume with sixteen essays and one interview with Shashi Deshpande offers a broad spectrum of her craft and concerns. Concentrating on individual text, the essays focus on her philosophical and existential concerns and relate them to issues of autonomy and selfhood, social activism, resistance and reconciliation in human relationships. Some of the essays focus on narrative and linguistic devices also.

Perhaps no full-length study has been made of Githa Hariharan. *Indian Women Novelists* edited by R.K. Dhawan set 3 vol. 4 (1995) has four essays on Githa Hariharan—"Penance as Multiple Response in Githa Hariharan's *The Thousand Faces of Night*" by Damodar Rao, "The Art of Fiction: A Note on the 'Prelude' of Githa Hariharan's *The Thousand Faces of Night*" by Rama Nair, Indira Nityanandam's "A Search for Identity: *The Thousand Faces of Night*" and "Walking the Tight Rope: A Reading of Githa Hariharan's *The Thousand Faces of Night*" by S. Indira. All of these essays confine themselves to one novel and talk about the feminist issues raised in the novel. A move away from this direction has been initiated by C. Vijayshree in "Re-Visionist Myth Making: A Reading of Githa Hariharan's *The Thousand Faces of Night*" included in *The Postmodern Indian English Novel* edited by Viney Kirpal (1996). The essay focuses on the rewriting of myths, but again the discussion is confined to one novel. *Gender and Narrative* edited by Jasbir Jain and Supriya Agarwal (2002) includes an essay by Dr Jasbir Jain "The Body in/of the Text: Structure and Meaning in Women's Narratives" which makes a comparative study of two short stories—Anjana Appachana's "Bahu" and Githa Hariharan's "The Remains of the Feast". The essay works through the category of gender.

Desert in Bloom edited by Meenakshi Bharat (2004) includes three essays on Hariharan. Rajeshwari Sunder Rajan's essay titled "The Heroine's Progress: Feminism and the Family in the fiction of Shashi Deshpande, Githa Hariharan and Manjula Padmanabhan" makes a comparative study of Shashi Deshpande's *That Long Silence*, Hariharan's *The Thousand Faces of Night* and Padmanabhan's *Hot Death, Cold Soup*. The essay traces the protagonist's progress to independence and identity, and the evolution of feminist awareness. Jasbir Jain's essay in the same volume titled "Men in the Minds of Women" probes the reasons for the choice of a male narrator in women writers' works and the allied movement to and androgynous writing. Focusing on shared experiences between the male and female in Desai's *In custody*, Sehgal's *Mistaken Identity* and Hariharan's *The Ghost of Vasu Master*, she maintains that there is something in the subject matter that dictates the choice of a male narrator. *Studies in Women Writers in English* edited by Mohit K. Ray and Rama Kundu, which contains nineteen essays, covers a wide spectrum of women writers across space and time. Of these, the two are on Githa Hariharan. The one by Arpita Mukhopadhyay, which focuses on mother-daughter relationship in *The Thousand Faces of Night*, brings out perceptively Githa Hariharan's handling of the age-old form of oral narration. Jaydeep Rishi examines Hariharan's later novel *When Dreams Travel*, and reads it as the 'daughter's quest for a literary mother'.

By and large, the major focus has been on themes like quest for identity, feminist assertion and modes of resistance. Equally and perhaps more significant would be to see how, working through historical and traditional contexts, they have raised several issues of contemporary India, their use of myth, fable and the *Upanishads* through which they open the texture of social thought and their contribution to the narrative form which has ushered in conspicuous changes in the scope and art of the novel. In the following chapters an attempt has been made in these directions.

References

Carr, E.H. *What is History*. New York: Knopf, 1961.

Deshpande, Shashi. "Where Do We Belong", *Writing from the Margin and Other Essays*. New Delhi: Penguin, 2003.

——. "In Conversation with Gita Viswanath", *Writing Difference: The Novels of Shashi Deshpande*. Ed. Chanchala K. Naik. New Delhi: Pencraft, 2005.

——. "Writing and Activism", *Writing Difference: The Novels of Shashi Deshpande*. Ed. Chanchala K. Naik. New Delhi: Pencraft,2005.

Hariharan, Githa. "A New take on Power", Interview with Anuradha Marwah Rao. *Pioneer*,7/2/1999.

——. "Discreet Thoughts", *Desert in Bloom*. Ed. Meenakshi Bharat. New Delhi: Pencraft, 2004.

——. "In Conversation with Arnab Chakladar". 5 August 2006 <http://www.anothersubcontinent.com/gh 1.html.

Jain, Jasbir. *Beyond Postcolonialism: Dreams and Realities of a Nation*. Jaipur and Delhi: Rawat Publications, 2006.

James, Henry. "The Art of Fiction", *The House of Fiction*. Ed. Leon Edel. London: Mercury Books, 1962.

Jenkins, Keith. *On What is History? From Carr and Elton to Rorty and White*. London, 1995.

Kakar, Sudhir. *The Inner World: A Psycho-analytic of Childhood and Society in India*. New Delhi: OUP, 2002.

Levi-Strauss, Claud. *The Savage Mind*. London: Weidenfeld & Nicolson, 1996.

Price, Reynolds. *A Palpable God: Thirty Stories Translated from the Bible*. New York: Atheneum, 1978.

Ramanujan, A.K. "Three Hundred Ramayanas", *The Collected Essays of A.K. Ramanujan*. Ed. Vinay Dharwadker. New Delhi: OUP, 2004.

Rege, Josna E. "Victim into Protagonist? *Midnight's Children* and the Post-Rushdie National Narratives of the English", *Rushdie's Midnight's Children: A Book of Readings*. Ed. Meenakshi Mukherjee. Delhi: Pencraft International, 2003.

Rushdie, Salman. *Midnight's Children*. London: Jonathan Cape, 1981.

Slemon, Stephen. "Post–Colonial Allegory and the Transformation of History". *Journal of Commonwealth Literature*, Vol. 23, No. 1, 1988.

Tharoor, Shashi. *The Great Indian Novel*. New Delhi: Penguin, 1989.

Watt, Ian. *The Rise of the Novel*. Berkeley: University of California Press, 1959.

Williams, Raymond. "Realism and Contemporary Novel", *Twentieth Century Literary Criticism*. Ed. David Lodge. London: Longman, 1972.

Woolf, Virginia. "The Modern Fiction", *Twentieth Century Literary Criticism*. Ed. David Lodge. London: Longman, 1972.

CHAPTER 2

Mythological Stories

The word 'myth', as Richard Chase in "Notes on the Study of Myths" (1974) points out, is a powerful word but not precise and as such eludes any single definition or interpretation. At one simple level it can be seen as a story, at another level and a more complicated one, it is a cultural reality that continues from one generation to another. According to A.H. Abrams:

> A myth is one story in a *mythology*—a system of hereditary stories which were once believed to be true by a particular cultural group and which served to explain (in terms of the intentions and actions of supernatural beings) why the world is as it is and things happen as they do and to establish the rationale for social customs and observances and the sanctions for the rules by which men conduct their lives. (2001: 102)

It is also worthwhile to know what the well-known anthropologist Malinowski has to say about myth. In his opinion:

> Myth is a vital ingredient of human civilisation; it is not an idle tale, but a hard-worked active force; it is not an intellectual explanation or artistic imagery, but a pragmatic charter of primitive faith and moral wisdom .... These stories do not live by idle interest; they are not narrated as historical accounts of ordinary facts. They are to the natives a statement of a higher and more important truth of a primeval reality which is still regarded as the foundation of present day life. (2002: 23)

Both the definitions, besides making several other points, stress one thing and that is that though myths may have taken their origin in the remote past, they continue to be of great significance to that particular society to which they are culturally relevant. The social and ethical norms codified in these myths regulate the actions and behaviour of the people of that society, not only that, they are often judged by those norms. It is for this reason that the writers invariably draw on myths as they provide the framework by which the culture of a society and its relationship with the individual can be understood and interpreted. The use of myths also facilitates the writer to bring the past and the present together which further enables him/her to view reality in the larger temporal perspective. One more reason is their flexibility which provides the author the possibility of a whole range of interpretations. In "Myth, Fiction, and Displacement" Northrop Frye, emphasising the creative and flexible nature of myths, writes:

> No rendering of any myth into conceptual language can serve as a full equivalent of its meaning. A myth may be told or retold, it may be modified or elaborated, or different patterns may be discovered in it and its life is always the poetic life of a story, not the homiletic life of some of illustrated truism. (1974: 165)

Richard Chase also rejects the idea of myth as a body of dogma or a worldview, or as a 'canon of behaviour or thought'.

Retaining the meaning of the Greek word 'myth' which means story, he writes in "Notes on the Study of Myths":

> The fact is that the simplest meaning of the Greek word "myth" is the right one: *a myth is a story, myth is narrative or poetic literature*. Myth is therefore art and must be studied as such. Myth is a mode of cognition, a system of thought, a way of life, only as art is. (1974: 245)

In the essay Chase stresses that literature should be brought closer to myth and feels that the work of Eliot, Yeats, Mann, Joyce and others have been able to take only tentative steps towards 'the search for myth'. Although the use of mythology is something that writers in all ages have taken resort to, most of the writers in the twentieth century have embodied Chase's views in their works and have employed them in a variety of ways. Michael Bell in "Anthropology and/as Myth in Modern Criticism" points out that earlier writers made a 'literary' use of myths whereas writers in the 20th century, to be more specific, towards the end of it, have combined literary, philosophical and psychological motives in their use of myths. Not only that, there is an assimilation of contemporary anthropological conceptions also. Consequently, both in literature and anthropology myth has become, to quote Michael Bell, "a less numinous and more workday category" (2006: 128).

It is being increasingly realised that myths have their origin in a particular socio-cultural context and so when the context changes, they need to be re-interpreted and sometimes even significantly modified. This realisation has led to a rewriting of myths in terms of contemporary situations which has replaced their 'metaphysical and universalistic claims by cultural, historical specificity'. In the context of India this becomes all the more necessary as the myths in the two epics, the *Ramayana* and the *Mahabharata*, are a part of collective consciousness and exert a continuous and pervasive influence on the minds of Indian people. This is not merely because, as Shashi Deshpande points out, "the past always seems more glorious to us, but it is also because so many of the values embodied in these two epics are still deeply embedded in us" (2003: 199). Elaborating upon this point, she writes:

> A Ram or a Sita, a Krishna or a Arjuna, a Draupadi or a Savitri- these are not just characters in stories to us; they are as real as the people around us. Loving brothers are still a Ram-Laxman, an ideal couple is still a Ram-Sita or a Laxmi-Narayan ... And words like 'Laxman Rekha' or 'Vanvas' because of their origin and association with the old stories, carry a weight of meaning, which, most of those who are familiar with the stories, would immediately comprehend. (2003: 88)

Undoubtedly, myths are an integral part of our lives. They define a society's religious beliefs, historical traditions and comprise in themselves the fundamental conventions of culture and interpersonal relationships. Also, at the same time, they bind the members of a group to each other and forge a collective identity making it separate and distinct from the collective identities of other groups. But the problem begins when they are interpreted dogmatically or allegorically. Emphasising the seminal nature of myths, Philip Slater writes, "Myths is an elaborately condensed product, that there is no one 'correct' version or interpretation, for no matter how many layers one peels off, there will remain much to be explained" (cited in Kakar, 2002: 66). The *Ramayana* and the *Mahabharata* are in themselves complex texts which can be interpreted in various ways. The *Ramayana*, as Jasbir Jain in *Gendered Realities* points out, can be read 'as a discourse on hierarchy, relationships, good and evil behaviour and also as a dialogue between the 'self' and the 'other'' (2003: 100). Similarly, the *Mahabharata* is replete with legal debates. We find dilemmas; questions and situations that we are often faced with and to which it offers answers but no answer is offered with finality. In this connection, Iravati Karve writes in *Yuganta*:

> Nowhere else does one find so many discussions about what is Dharma and what is not as in the *Mahabharata*. In works like the *Bible* and the *Quran* there is a categorical statement what religion consists in. In the *Mahabharata* there are questions, answers and doubts regarding the nature of religion and human destiny. That is the reason why the story comes so close to us. (1994: 195)

The great tradition embodied in these two epics can be used variedly but, as Githa Hariharan points out in "New Voices: New Challenges", these texts have been viewed as "documented history and the complexity of each myth and legend and folk tale has been shrunk to one safe authoritative expression" (*Littcrit*: 10). The characters in these myths have been reduced to stereotypes rather than seen as complex questioning characters. Culturally Sita is seen as the very soul of unquestioning acceptance. Her show of strength, when she refused to prove her chastity with the second ordeal by fire and disappeared into the receiving arms of her mother leaving no room for negotiations, has not been emphasised either by religion or by culture. This is pointed out by Jasbir Jain in *Gendered Realities*:

> In fact, if one reads the 'Uttara Kanda' carefully, it is evident that she is sacrificed to Ram's own pursuit of perfection. He wishes to be without fault and above all men. And as the forces of nature gather together to protect Sita, they silently pass a judgement on Ram and uphold the truth of Sita's life, who then emerges as a stronger woman. This aspect of her life is not emphasised either by religion or by popular culture. (2003: 100)

The *Ramayana* and the *Mahabharata,* products as they are of the patriarchal culture, they are men-oriented and have looked at the world from a man's point of view. This man-centred point of view goes on to privilege male over the female. Ram, to quote Kakar, "may have all the traits of a godlike hero, yet he is also fragile, mistrustful and jealous and very much a conformist, both to his parents' wishes and to public opinion" (2002: 66). He is seen as 'Maryada Purshottam', one who epitomises tradition. In fact the roots of patriarchy, as Jasbir observes in her introduction to *Women in Patriarchy,* lie in the creation of these myths which has located itself in the power of men and subordination of women and so any questioning of patriarchal stronghold begins with the questioning of beliefs contained in these myths (2005: 13). Even the concept of 'dharma' is seen very differently for men and women. Shalmalee Palekar points out in "Gender, Feminism, Postcoloniality" how 'stridharma' revolves around the concept of 'pativrata' (2005: 65).

Writers writing about India cannot ignore such a reality and have invariably gone to the *Ramayana* and the *Mahabharata.* When it comes to the use of myths in writers like Shashi Deshpande and Githa Hariharan, they have mostly seen them from the consciousness of a woman who strongly feels that old roles are no longer relevant or feasible in changing social and political conditions. An ideal woman is still seen as Sita, supported by other figures like Savitri, Draupadi and Gandhari. "To be as pure as Sita, as loyal as Draupadi, as dogged in devotion as Savitri, as beautiful as Laxmi, as bountiful a provider as Annapurna, as strong as Durga—these have become the ultimate role models for women" (Deshpande, 2003: 89). Society's expectations from a woman and a woman's own perception of herself have long been largely determined by the values embodied in these ideal figures. The tales of their sacrifice and single minded devotion learned from childhood make their way into the deeper layers of the Indian women's psyche and become so psychologically rooted that even when they reject these models, it is often accompanied by a sense of guilt within them. Shashi Deshpande points out that not only men but also women have taken their idea of a perfect woman from these myths:

> The fact is we don't start with a picture of ourselves on a clear slate. Already inscribed on this are things told to us by others, there is what we read, what we gather from the ideas and expectations around us, what we imagine and dream. Myths form a large part of this baggage we bring to our self image. How we see ourselves, collectively or individually, depends greatly on myths ... . (2003: 87)

Films and tele-serials also play an enormous role in fostering these ideas which cannot be easily weeded out as they have become a part of the way we think. In her introduction to *The Post Modern Novel*, Viney Kirpal refers to the constant use of the plot and characters from both the *Ramayana* and the *Mahabharata* and the positive and negative images of male and female which goes on to make simplified categorisation between good and evil (1996: 22).

There are several mythological stories embedded in the works of Shashi Deshpande and Githa Hariharan which they have taken from the *Ramayana* and the *Mahabharata* and one has to open them out in order to understand their works. They have used myths both for mediation and subversion to evolve an alternative or oppositional viewpoint as against the dominant one and in doing so they sever them from the age-old shackles of cultural hegemony. In addition to Shashi Deshpande and Githa Hariharan, this rewriting of myths is being done by several other Indian writers writing in English and other Indian languages. One name worth mentioning is that of Mahasweta Devi, a Bengali writer whose works have been translated into several languages. Her story titled 'Draupadi', translated into English by

Gayatri Spivak, is a retelling of the episode of the 'Chirharan' in the *Mahabharata*. Draupadi prays to Lord Krishna to protect her when Kauravas attempt to disrobe in the open court. In Mahasweta Devi's version, Draupadi, gang-raped by the police, refuses to be clothed by men again saying, "What is the use of clothes? You can strip me, but how can you clothe me again? Are you a man … . There isn't a man here that I should be ashamed. What more can you do? Come on, *kounter* me—come on, *kounter* me" (2002: 36–37).

Anjana Appachana's story "Bahu", included in *Incantations* (Penguin, 1991), subverts the ideal perpetuated through the story of the legendary Sita. The protagonist in the story has been married for some time. One evening she goes to see a movie with her husband and her in-laws. In the film the heroine, who is pregnant, is turned out of the house by her husband as she is suspected of having an affair with the villain. In the mean time her innocence is proved and so when she returns with her son, her husband accepts her by saying 'emotionally': "You are my Sita … . Even the Lord Rama abandoned his pregnant wife in the forest" (10). Unlike the heroine in the film or Sita of the *Ramayana*, the protagonist in Appachana's story walks out of her in-law's house when she realises that they have assumed complete control over her life. Her husband tries to persuade her to stay back: "Don't think I don't understand. But what can be done about it? This is the way things are. You have to learn to accept it" (26). But she rejects the submissive, self-effacing role of a 'Bahu' and decides never to come back.

The role models projected by the Sita/Savitri prototype are so deeply ingrained in the psyche of the Indian woman that the act of defiance carries within it a sense of guilt. This point is brought home very vividly in the story by Anjana Appachana: "There comes a time when it isn't such a small matter any more.

But, still overwhelmed with guilt, still determined to please, you succumb again. Imperceptibly, but irrevocably, you slide into the kind of life that is completely contrary to everything you believe in" (13). The communication that takes place between the protagonist and her mother-in-law, after they have watched the film, illustrates the role of films in perpetuating the ideals of sacrifice and devotion on the part of a woman. When she tells her mother-in-law that the heroine should not have gone back as she was misused, her mother-in-law replies, "really? But then you see, she was not like you. She was a simple girl. She did her duty" (11–12).

Vaidehi, a Kannada writer, has rewritten the story of Shakuntala which is originally in the *Mahabharata* and is later transformed into a play by Kalidasa. The story, translated by Jaswant Jadav as "An Afternoon with Shakuntala", is included in *Women Writing in India* (Oxford, 1993). The characters and incidents in Vaidehi's story are all from the original play, but the perspective shifts. In the play, king Dushyant does not recognise Shakuntala and rejects her publicly. The king's act is justified by making a curse responsible for his forgetting her. In the end they are reunited. Vaidehi retells the story as "a tale of forgetfulness concocted by a man", and goes on to say that the poet "with some story of a curse hid man's careless debauchery" (1991: 542). In Vaidehi's version, Shakuntala refuses to go back to the king, though she allows him take her son as his heir.

Shashi Deshpande has written a volume of short stories titled *The Stone Women and Other Stories* in which we find a reflection of her concern with myths which permeate her novels. She wrote the title story "Stone Women" after her visit to the Channakeshava temple of Belur. What struck her there was the way women had been carved on the walls of the temple. They were depicted as 'playful, joyous narcissistic creatures', a picture 'far removed from reality'. But her real journey into the

Mahabharata and the *Ramayana* with a new vision began, as she acknowledges in "Telling her Own Stories" included in *Writing from the Margin,* when she came across Iravati Karve's interpretation of the character of Bhishma in the *Yuganta.* Bhishma, who has always been regarded as the greatest and the most respected character in the epic, is seen by Iravati Karve as "a man who had shown utter callousness towards women" (1994: 16). This observation gives Deshpande a new insight, as she says in the essay. It inspired her to write the story "Inner Rooms". The story is a retelling of the story of Amba, the princess of Kashi, from the *Mahabharta.* She, along with her sisters, is carried away by Bhishma to marry his brother Vichitravirya after he has defeated the king of Salva in a personal combat. When Amba tells Bhishma that she is in love with the king of Salva, he sends her to him, but the king of Salva refuses to accept her as he has lost his claim on her by losing the combat. Amba, all doors closing on her, desperately turns to Bhishma asking him to marry her but he refuses as he has already taken a vow of celibacy. In the story, Amba has been seen as a rebel, strongly conscious of a personal sense of dignity, keen on getting married to a partner of her own choice, unwilling to enter into a loveless marriage. She emerges out as a woman capable of thinking and questioning. After this story Deshpande goes on to reinterpret stories from the *Mahabharata* and the *Ramayana.* Shashi Deshpande says that it was "like seeing people in pictures on the wall coming to life and walking out of them into mine" (2003: 91). In the story "And What Has Been Decided" Draupadi has been shown as a woman who discards her mythical shell and expresses her vexation and anguish at the delay and shift in Pandavas' decision regarding war even after she has been humiliated by the Kauravas in the court. Her protest in the story has its roots in her realisation that a woman's insult is taken lightly. In "Hear Me Sanjay" the story is told by Kunti, the mother of the Pandavas and is addressed to Sanjay who described the events of the battle to Dhritrashtra.

The story deconstructs the notion of glory attached with the practice of taking vows:

> What use was it blinding herself? Oh, these futile vows! I sometimes think they're just a cover for the willfulness of self-willed people. Look at Bhishma!. Do you remember those two queens, our mothers-in-law, Gandhari's and mine? ... *Oh,* Yes, vows, that's right, I was speaking of vows. You know, Sanjay sometimes I think—if only Bhishma had given up his vow, if he had had children of his own, then perhaps those sisters would have lived normal, happy lives. (150)

Gandhari destroyed her life by covering her eyes and Bhishma's vow of celibacy destroyed not only the life of Amba, but also the lives of her sisters; Ambika and Ambalika. They were deceived into sleeping with a stranger after the death of their husband Vichitravirya so that they could bear children to rule the kingdom.

The story "A Wall is Safer" has a subversive dimension to it. In the story Sita is the maid servant whose marital life has been full of sufferings. The name 'Sita' does not bring to her mind the image of an ideal wife. For her it is a name that brings misfortune: "what can you expect when you are named Sita Bai but misfortunes?" (65). "The Last Enemy" takes up several philosophical issues and works through Duryodhana's consciousness. The story begins after the Kauravas have lost the battle. Duryodhana is left alone after brothers are killed in the war. As he reviews his life at this point of time, he sees the futility of hankering after 'glory and dignity, power and magnificence'. He is disillusioned and sees loneliness and death as the only reality of life. The title of the story is significant. It is the desire for glory, prompted by ego, which, in fact is our enemy disguised as ambition and dream.

In this chapter, I propose to study in detail the mythological stories embedded in Shashi Deshpande's *That Long Silence* and

Githa Hariharan's *The Thousand Faces of Night*. The central thrust of both the novels has been placed against the backdrop of cultural myths. Myths provide the protagonists with a variety of situations to which they respond by negotiating them so that they can live both in normative and subversive ways. The novels also encapsulate the tension that emerges from the conflict between a woman's desire to perform and the necessity to conform to socially desired and approved pattern of life.

That Long Silence begins with an upheaval in the life of Jaya, the protagonist. Her husband Mohan gets implicated in business malpractices in his job and there is an inquiry against him. The two move out from their permanent residence at Churchgate to a house at Dadar in Bombay till things come back to normal. This shift offers Jaya a break from the monotonous and tiring routine as the children are away on a tour and Mohan does not have to go to office. Consequently, it also gives her time and opportunity to reflect on her life. Her acquiescence in her husband's plan to shift to Dadar flat reminds her of the mythical Sita who followed Ram when he was exiled:

> I remember now that he had assumed I would accompany him, had taken for granted my acquiescence in his plans so had I. Sita following her husband into exile, Savitri dogging Death to reclaim her husband, Draupadi stoically sharing her husband's travails. (11)

The references to Sita; Savitri and Draupadi, as Jasbir Jain observes, "construct the image of *pativrata*, a woman who places her devotion above all else. Each reference individually spells out a wife's duty, no matter how unfair or unjust the husband's treatment of her may have been" (2003: 228). Deshpande makes Jaya fall back upon these mythical figures in her relationship with her husband for two reasons. Firstly, to show that the ideal of womanhood incorporated by these figures still governs the inner world of a woman and exerts a continuous pressure on her existence and secondly to deconstruct the mythic past as Jaya goes on to view marriage as a relationship in which the husband and the wife are 'yoked together':

> No. What have I to do with these mythical women? I can't fool myself. The truth is simpler. Two bullocks yoked together ... It is more comfortable for them to move in the same direction. To go in different directions would be painful, and what animal would voluntarily choose pain? (11–12)

The image of the 'two bullocks yoked together' performing their duty mechanically subverts the myth of the merging of the two bodies into one in a marriage. Later in the novel, Jaya rejects this image also as it leaves no room for options or alternatives.

Though Jaya follows Mohan for she knows that going in a different direction would be difficult, she follows him resentfully. In *The Dark Holds No Terrors* also, the stories of Sita and Draupadi are called up in a similar context when Sarita; the protagonist says that Sita and Draupadi consciously abandoned their independent identities as living their lives the way they lived was an easier and more comfortable way of survival. They chose to "swim along the tide and not against the tide for the fear of the struggle" (137). Jaya takes this decision of following Mohan as she was 'scared of jeopardizing the only career she had, her marriage' which offered her 'security', a security which could dwindle at any attempt of self-assertion" (144).

The myth of Sita following Ram is exploded further in an unexpected way when Jaya sees herself and her husband as "a man and a woman climbing the dingy stairs of a drab building in the heart of Bombay" (7). As they reach the closed door of the flat, Mohan holds out his hand for keys, but Jaya ignores him. He continues to stand there for a moment with his hand held out in a 'supplicatory gesture', and then follows her.

Jaya goes through her diaries which she has written earlier and in them she has referred to herself as 'Mohan's wife, Rahul's and Rati's mother and not herself' (170). The diaries are nothing but painstaking entries of items bought, dates of children's schools and insurance payments. The record reflects her career as a wife and mother and what is left out is the existence of Jaya outside these roles. She ironically calls them 'The Diaries of a Sane Housewife' (70).

The ghosts of the past Jaya is confronted with, continue to prod her memory and remind her how her career as a writer has been constrained in several ways. She had written a story which won her the first prize in a competition. The story was about a couple—a man who could reach out to his wife only through her body. Though the story won the first prize Mohan was not happy with it as he thought that the man in the story might be identified with him. He propelled Jaya into other kind of writing because the women in the kind of writing she had done earlier might, says Jaya ironically, "resemble Mohan's mother, or aunt or my mother or aunt." (149). She had to take up writing a column entitled 'Seeta' in which she wrote light, humorous stories about "the travails of middle class housewives" (144).

Shashi Deshpande has deliberately named the column 'Seeta' so as to invest it with mythic resonance and by doing so she reveals the stronghold of the values projected by myths on the minds of the people. Mohan loved the column and so did the editors and the readers and for Jaya it was a 'safe hole in which she could stay warm and snug' (149). Jaya now realises, as she reflects retrospectively, that by writing the column 'Seeta', she had shut out the silent, suffering women clamouring for attention. She remembers how she had 'relinquished' all those stories that had been taking shape in her mind for fear of hurting Mohan, of putting her marriage in danger. She had thought that she would be safe, but now she realises that "safety is always unattainable. You are never safe" (17). With this realisation, she gives up the 'Seeta' column. Jaya's giving up of the 'Seeta' column is symbolic. She refuses to remain under the protective shadows of characters like Sita or Savitri:

> Suddenly Seeta had exploded, there was nothing left of her, not even bits and pieces that could be put together. It gave me pleasure to think of the blank age where Seeta would have been but of course there would be no blank page there never could be one. There would be something replacing Seeta and I had to search for it. (69)

The crisis in Mohan's career distances Jaya from the image of wifehood and motherhood that has accumulated over millennia of use and which she had tried to live up to. Now she begins to see herself in a totally different perspective. She recalls that she has had a name also—Suhasini, the name given to her by Mohan on their wedding. As Suhasini is like Sita, the woman of the 'Seeta' column, "a soft, smiling, placid, motherly woman", Jaya rejects Suhaasini as well (15). It is also a manifestation of protest against such customs.

Jaya invokes the story of Gandhari also in an entirely different context which creates a mock epic effect. She had never tried to find out how Mohan got a job in Bombay and how he got everything that they had needed. In that way she had 'bandaged' her eyes tightly. She ironically says "if Gandhari, who bandaged her eyes to become blind like her husband, could be called an ideal wife, I was an ideal wife too" (61). By bringing the two stories together, Deshpande has exploded the myth of Gandhari's sacrifice. In this connection Jasbir Jain observes, "Whether Gandhari, did so out of her sense of wifely devotion or out of resentment for having been cheated into marrying a blind man, it is difficult to say" (2003: 228). In *The Binding Vine* also myth has been subverted through experiential reality. In the novel Mira, who is a writer, is married to a man who cannot think of her beyond her body and to whom she has to submit unwillingly. She writes a poem which subverts the myth of the divine couple Lakshmi-Narayna.: "But tell me, friend, did Laxmi too/twist brocade tassels round her fingers/and tremble fearing the coming/of the dark-clouded, engulfing night?" (66). The image which stands for marital happiness is transformed into something which comes nearer to her own experience of sex and marriage.

Jaya, who has been unquestioning till now, rejects her role of Gandhari. She prefers to be like Maitreyee, the sage Yajnavalkya's wife who rejected her husband's offer of half of his property and instead asked him, "Will this property give me immortality?" (25). By assuming the role of Maitreyee, Jaya is, as Naresh K. Jain points out, "seeking strength from a more vital part of our tradition in order to move towards greater autonomy and greater mutuality" (1998: 15).

As Jaya revisits her life through "the disorderly, chaotic, sequence of events and non-events" of her life, she finds it was "like looking through the eyehole of the magic peepshow" (187). It was a journey into her own 'self' and at the end of this journey she finds herself looking at the picture of "a girl, a child wearing a dress with pockets for the first time, thrusting her hands in them, feeling heady with the excitement of finding unexpected resources within herself" (187). The realisation dawns upon her: "*That child was me*. With this discovery comes another thought. *I will begin with her, with this child*" (187). The meaning is figurative. She now decides to begin a new life in which there will be a space for her own 'self'. At the end of the novel, as Kalidas Misra writes in "Writing a Narrative and a Self in Silence", "We find Jaya as a fully evolved self, prepared to live a life different from the one articulated through the character of Sita and Suhaasini … . If she is still the same Mohan's wife, she refuses to succumb to any prescribed role model and would not tolerate any attempt to circumscribe or inhibit her life" (2005: 76). Jaya emerges as an integrated person, a woman who can speak for herself in her own language. Earlier she had 'cut off the bits of her that had refused to be Mohan's wife', but she realises that this kind of a fragmentation is not possible (191). Towards the end she recalls Lord Krishna's words to Arjun from the *Bhagwad Geeta* which allows room for the realisation of the human will: "I have given you knowledge. Now you make the choice. The choice is yours. Do as you desire" (192). This, however, does not imply abdication of one's duties and obligations. What Shashi Deshpande is emphasising here is the need to carve out a little space for one's own self. Jaya discovers a sense of freedom, not by giving up, but by formulating her sense of responsibility to her husband and children anew. As Shalmalee Palekar puts it, "the issues of tradition and modernity are set against each other and shown to exist on a continuum rather than being completely oppositional and in which the concept of freedom is qualified" (2005: 65).

Githa Hariharan's *The Thousand Faces of Night* interweaves stories of three women, Devi; the protagonist, Sita; her mother and Mayamma, the old maidservant, each belonging to different generations. The stories are interwoven with the stories of mythological figures and once the myths come into the narrative, the stories acquire another level of significance. Githa Hariharan herself tells us:

> I used this approach to enlarge the limited space of women's lives. The background of the mythical figures from Sita to Kali can help us to understand Indian women's lives, instead of just seeing that they are hammed in. (2004: 380)

When the novel *The Thousand Faces of Night* opens, Devi is in America and has already decided to go back to India. Her character has been shaped by the many mythological stories told her by her grandmother in her childhood. In her grandmother's stories, the heroines always grew up safe with the knowledge that they would have a noble and loving prince and the stories always ended on a happy note. Devi, then a small impressionable girl, filled her mind with the fantasy that she too would live like a princess and was excited at the 'splendours' that awaited her. During her stay in America, she received proposals of marriage but they could not move her as they failed to re-conjure 'the myth-laden' world that had been absorbed in the past. Refusing an offer of marriage from her black American friend Dan, she returns to India.

Once Devi is in India, her mother asks her to forget about the experiences she has had in America and prepares her for marriage. At this point of life, she is reminded of her grandmother's stories of 'pre-destined husbands' and 'idyllic marriages'. Her grandmother had told her the story of Nala and Damyanti and their *'Swayamvara'* with all 'its solemnity and royal dignity'. The whole situation is reversed when Devi is married to Mahesh who is no prince but a Regional Manager and that too in a detergent company. Her dream world is shattered and she is happy that her grandmother is no longer alive: "I am glad she is not here to see me at my *'Swayamvara'*, the princess' robe she lovingly stitched for me" (20). The whole idea of *'Swayamvara'*, which carries with it the idea of the bride's choice, collapses. She realises that in arranging a marriage it is not the bride's choice that matters. On the contrary, the decision rests with the boy and his family.

Mahesh has a very practical approach to marriage and views it as just another necessity. Devi thinks if she is going to play out a travesty of myths that had filled her childhood, it would be better to cast aside all pretence and be as matter of fact as Mahesh. She moves from a romantic idea of love to a more realistic view of their relationship.

Devi gradually realises that her grandmother's stories were like 'the sugar shapes' she made for her, "a rich oversweet syrup that was magically transformed over the fire with ornamented little elephants, swans with each feather delicately etched, her stories fashioned moulds. Ideal moulds, impossibly ambitious ..." (27). The grandmother always chose a mythological story for a particular occasion for she thought there was a vital link between her stories and real life, though she could not always find a precise mythological story for every real-life situation that confronted her. Devi recalls how her grandmother had tried to link the story of Gandhari with that of her mother, Sita. On one occasion, Devi found an old studio photograph in which her mother was holding a *veena*. She asked her grandmother if her mother played the *veena*. In reply to Devi's question, the grandmother first narrated the story of Gandhari which she summed up by saying, "She embraced her destiny—a blind husband—with a sacrifice worthy of her royal blood" (29) and then came to the story of Devi's mother. She told Devi that when Sita was married, she brought with her a *veena* that she had received as part of her dowry. She played it everyday after she had finished her household duties and played it so beautifully that the eyes of those who listened to her brimmed with tears. But one day her father-in-law could not find some thing he needed. He called out to Sita but as she was playing *veena*, she could not hear him. He got infuriated and said: "put that *veena* away. Are you a wife, a daughter-in-law" (30). Sita remained silent for some time and then broke the strings of the *veena* saying: "yes I am a wife, a daughter-in-law" (30). After this incident she never touched the *veena* again and became a 'dutiful' housewife.

This act of Devi's mother Sita is taken by her grandmother as an act of sacrifice and she links it with the story of Gandhari which has been culturally interpreted as a tale of sacrifice. Hariharan gives another version of the story through Devi. Devi could see that it was not a sacrifice, but Gandhari's anger at having been duped into marrying a blind man that became the central motive of years of blind suffering and it is in this way that her mother's story and Gandhari's story come together. Sita's act of pulling out the strings of the *veena* with a vow never to touch it again was not an act of sacrifice but an act of protest against her father-in-law's accusations.

In the novel Sita becomes a dutiful wife and a daughter-in-law whom everybody praises. Though, ostensibly, she reflects the socially moulded image of the mythical Sita, Hariharan goes on to counteract that image. Sita's wifely role gives her a sense of power. She rules the household territory with 'an iron hand' taking decisions for her husband and her daughter. She works for her husband's advancement, leading him like a "conductor than an accompanist" (103). Both Devi and her father allow themselves to be ruled by her, though not without resentment. She does not allow them to indulge in any kind of dreams and calls the stories of gods and goddesses 'fairy tales'. The wifely devotion of the mythical Sita is illustrated through Sita of the novel, only to be exploded further. Though she succeeds in reaching her goal of wifehood with relentless self discipline, she distances herself from her husband and her daughter. Her husband dies alone as if he does not want to share even his last struggle with her. She finds him dead in his room with his head resting on a pile of papers on his desk. In a very mechanical way, she lifts his head, pulls out the papers and burns them before the body is cremated which symbolises that she has done away with him and her memories of him.

Devi can now see that an ordinary real woman like her mother cannot always rise to the heroic proportions of her grandmother's version of Gandhari's sacrifice. She now recalls all the mythological stories as told to her by her grandmother and sees the cracks in the bridge her grandmother had built between those stories and the real-life stories. She is reminded of the story of her cousin Uma which propelled her grandmother to relate the story of Amba from the *Mahabharata*. Uma was a motherless child. When she got married all were happy as her in-laws were very wealthy. But all her dreams were shattered. Her father-in-law and her husband 'drank' till late in the night and they drank so much that she was terrified of them. Even an unhappy childhood, with an indifferent father and a hostile stepmother, had not prepared her for this trial and the things reached beyond her tolerance when her father-in-law tried to molest her. She left the house and came to live with Devi's grandmother. Devi, then a small girl, questioned her grandmother persistently about Uma and her brief marriage. The grandmother tried to comfort her by saying:

> Ah, Devi why weep over Uma? A high-born princess or even a goddess has been the victim of disaster. But a woman like Amba, a truly courageous woman, finds the means to transform her hatred, the fate that overtakes her, into a triumph. (36)

Though the grandmother had narrated the story of Amba as the story of a woman who turned her misfortune into triumph Devi; now grown up, knows the difference that lies between the strength of Amba and a mere human being like Uma.

As Devi probes into her life and the lives of her mother and Mayamma; the domestic help, she finds similarities in experiences but difference in responses. Each of them has walked the tight rope and struggled for some balance, for some means of survival they could design for themselves. Mayamma, born two generations before Devi, suffers bestial cruelty at the hands of her husband and mother-in-law and later her spoilt son. Though she is ill-humoured she has no bitterness. Sita, born fifteen years after Mayamma, is different. Her survival, a generation away from Mayamma, has been far more efficient than Mayamma's but Devi can feel her relentless pain and emptiness in her ruthless attempts to keep her ambitions at bay. Devi tries to fit herself in the role of a wife and a daughter-in-law as her mother has done years ago but she feels trapped in that role. Whenever she feels a desire to do something she really wants like learning Sanskrit or taking up a job or at least learning to play cards, her husband disapproves. She is confronted with an emptiness threatening her very existence. She then takes refuge in her father-in-law's stories of 'virtuous' wives who have been instrumental in making their husbands walk on the spiritual path. Fed on the stories of virtuous wives, she tries to vanquish all her desires but fails to bridge the gap between her and Mahesh. Subsequently, the marriage loses all its meanings when she fails to have a child.

Devi thinks of humiliating Mahesh, to do "something bloody, final, a mark of protest worthy of the heroines she grew up with" (95). She sees herself sometimes as Kali-Durga in her dreadful form and at other times as Devi, the benevolent goddess 'above mortal indignities and cravings'. She tries endless variations but they all "reek of cliché and platitude" (95). Defying them all, she walks out of the marriage. This act of Devi's is not an abdication of responsibility but an effort to reframe it outside the framework of an oppressive marriage and compulsory motherhood because, as Jasbir Jain has stated, "her life as a wife can be rendered functional only if she obliterates all else" (2004: 54).

When Devi's mother, Sita hears about it she is shocked. It is an unexpected betrayal for which she is not prepared. But then like a well grown hardy cactus which is untouched by sudden change in weather, she recoils from this shock and emerges as a stronger woman, determined to begin a new life. She waits for her daughter, Devi to return home. She also dusts the broken *veena* which is indicative of the fact that she will resume playing it. We find a parallel situation in the *Ramayana* when Sita refuses to go through a second ordeal by fire and disappears into the arms of her mother earth. Sita then emerges as a stronger woman.

In the novel, there is also the story of Parvati; Devi's mother-in-law, interwoven with the mythological story of Shiva and Parvati; the divine couple who represent the most successful marriage. The story is told to Devi by Mayamma. She tells Devi that her father-in-law married Parvati because "it was an old reliable name" (62). He had rejected other proposals as the names of the other girls were 'Hema' and 'Mohana' which sounded like "back-chatting tantrum throwing, modern girls" (62). What is most ironical in the story is that the man, who had always told stories of virtuous women who had been instrumental in initiating their husbands into sainthood, is deserted by his wife in her search of God. In the mythological story of Shiva and Parvati also, it was Parvati who had initiated Shiva into becoming a 'yogi' while she took charge of the household working at her marriage like any other mortal woman. But in the novel Parvati turns the story upside down as she gives up the life of a householder. Here Githa Hariharan also seeks to deconstruct the conventional glory which is attached to the act of desertion by men who are claimed to have done so for their pursuit of sainthood and the family is left behind to struggle, more so when the family is economically dependent on them.

Thus, we see that both Shashi Deshpande and Githa Hariharan have brought our ancient myths 'to our reality'. Past is seen not as static but in a state of constant flux which achieves simultaneity with the present as they go on to incorporate it by reshaping it. Multiple realities emerge as against the authoritative one. The merging of the personal into mythical and the collective in both the novels has made the narrative questioning and not descriptive.

References

Abrams, A.H. *A Glossary of Literary Terms*. New Delhi: Macmillan, 2001.

Appachana, Anjana. "Bahu", *Incantations and Other Stories*. New Delhi: Penguin, 1991.

Bell, Michael. "Anthropology and/as Myth in Modern Criticism", *Literary Theory and Criticism*. Ed. Patricia Waugh. Delhi: OUP, 2006.

Chase, Richard. "Notes on the Study of Myths", *Twentieth Century Criticism*. Ed. William J. Handy and Max Westbrook. New Delhi: Light and Life Publishers, 1974.

Deshpande, Shashi. "A Toppling Worldview", *Writing From the Margin*. New Delhi: Penguin, 2003.

——. "Telling Our Own Stories", *Writing From the Margin*. New Delhi: Penguin, 2003.

Devi, Mahasweta. "Draupadi", *Breast Stories*. Trans. by Gayatri Spivak, Kolkata: Seagull, 2002.

Hariharan, Githa."New Voices: New Challenges". *Littcrit*, Vol. 30, No. 1, June 2004.

——. "How I Write and Why? Githa Hariharan Answers", *Of Narratives and Narrators*. Eds. Rajul Bhargava and Shubhshree. New Delhi Jaipur: Rawat Publications, 2004.

Jain, Jasbir. *Gendered Realities, Human Spaces: The Writing of Shashi Deshpande*. Jaipur and New Delhi: Rawat Publications, 2003.

Jain, Naresh K. "Tradition, Modernity and Change", *Women in Indo Anglian Fiction*. Ed. Naresh K. Jain, New Delhi: Manohar Publishers, 1998.

Kakar, Sudhir. *The Inner World: A Psycho-analytic Study of Childhood and Society in India*, New Delhi: OUP, 2002.

Karve, Iravati. *Yuganta: The End of an Epoch*. Mumbai: Orient Longman, 1994.

Kirpal, Viney. *The Postmodern Novel*. Mumbai: Allied Publishers, 1996.

Malinowski, Bronislaw. *Myth in Primitive Psychology* (rpt., originally pub. in 1927). London: Routledge, 2002.

Misra, Kalidas. "Writing a Narrative and Self in Silence", *Writing Difference: The Novels of Shashi Deshpande*. Ed. Chanchala K. Naik, New Delhi: Pencraft International, 2005.

Paleker, Shalmalee. "Gender, Feminism and Postcoloniality: A Reading of Shashi Deshpande's Novels", *Writing Difference: The Novels of Shashi Deshpande*. Ed. Chanchala K. Naik. New Delhi: Pencraft International, 2005.

Vaidehi(Janaki Srinivas Murthy). "An Afternoon with Shakuntala" (originally in Kannada, translated. by Jaswant Jadav), *Women Writing in India*. Eds. Susie Tharu and K. Lalita. Vol. 2, Delhi: OUP, 1991.

CHAPTER 3

Real-Life Stories

Both Shashi Deshpande and Githa Hariharan believe that writers have a social and political responsibility to discharge. Since writers are citizens like everyone else, they should not or cannot remain at a distance from the world around them. Githa Hariharan emphasises that her life as a citizen comes before her life as a writer, a role she is so passionate about when she says:

> I am a writer, but I also live in modern India, and I am very much an engaged citizen of our multicultural society. So it is inevitable that I am interested in examining certain relevant themes. The tussles between tradition and modernity or better still, the making of modernity, equal rights for women in the arenas of legislation as well as social practice, and in recent times, the strengthening of secular ideas and movements to combat growing fundamentalism. Even if a writer does not write what is usually perceived as political writing—direct

> social commentary, or unbending realism or something authentically Indian—the writer should aim at revealing truths, questions and/or answers that are fundamentally political. Fiction has a thousand ways of giving us a new take on the dynamics of power relations. (2004: 214–215)

Hariharan firmly believes that political attitudes must come through in the writing and a good writer is not someone who is writing something perfect but someone who can meet the challenges of the times. Shashi Deshpande too holds that a writer, since she is supposed to have a greater sensibility, cannot ignore the social and political realities of the society in which she lives. In her writings there may not be a direct comment on the events that have actually taken place, she delineates the effects of those events on the people. In this connection, she writes:

> There was a time when I was scornful of what is called committed writing. I considered such writing flawed because its being message oriented diminishes its artistic worth. But now I know that all good writing is a socially committed writing, it comes out of a concern for the human predicament. I believe, as Camus says, that the greatness of an artist is measured by the balance the writer maintains between the values of creations and values of humanities. (1998: 36)

The major upheavals that have taken place in the last few years have touched both Shashi Deshpande and Githa Hariharan and they surface in their writing in one way or the other. Both are anguished to see the fabric of society being torn apart in the name of caste, religion and language. In "Writing and Activism", Shashi Deshpande writes: "I am frightened by the way the idea of this country as one of multiplicities is being eroded, of how slowly the idea is being circulated of a country of one people, one religion etc." (2005: 32). In her essay "In Times of Siege: Shrinking Spaces in Times of Globalisation", Githa Hariharan also expresses a similar concern. She writes that the same situation may have been faced in the past by many others in many places but "the contemporary faces of violence, hatred and exclusion are, unfortunately, unique in our times" (*Littcrit*: 36–37). Both the writers have examined these issues through their writings.

There are several stories embedded in the novels of both Shashi Deshpande and Githa Hariharan which are based on real-life stories. In Githa Hariharan's *In Times of Siege*, which takes up the rise of fundamentalism, there are several stories, included and referred to, both from history and contemporary life. In "A Meet-the Author Event" organised by Penguin Books India and the British Council, Nirmala Lakshman, the joint editor of *The Hindu*, describes it as a book that "chillingly reflects the realities of India with the brutalizing processes and the self-destructive tendencies set in motion in our society today" (on line version). The novel looks unflinchingly into the ugliness of ideological polarisation and sectarian conflict that has permeated every facet of life in India in recent years resulting in the shrinkage of space for free expression and free debate. To make her point Githa Hariharan has juxtaposed two ages, the Virasaiva Movement of the twelfth century led by Basava, and the sixteenth century routing of the Vijaya Nagar empire with the current rise of the fundamentalism forming the subtexts in the novel. This goes on to establish both continuities and discontinuities between the past and the present.

In the novel Shiv Murthy, who is a professor in an open university, becomes the target of fundamentalists. He has written a lesson on Basavanna, also called Basava; a twelfth century poet and social reformer, who believed that the Hindus' rigid and oppressive caste system needed radical reforming. The lesson is denounced by an organisation called 'Itihas Suraksha Manch' because Shiv has not "sung enough of a paean to the glory of Hindu kingdoms and also because he has made "too much of caste divisions among Hindus" (55). The 'Manch' also objects to Shiv's 'humanizing' of Basava whom it considers as a saint. Githa Hariharan writes ironically:

> The group is called the 'Itihas Suraksha Manch'. The protector of history, whoever heard of history having to be protected? It is true that whether people are talking about culture or history or women's rights, protection has become a much abused word. A cover up for all kinds of bullying tactics. (55)

The Head of the Department Mr Sharma, a timid person whose policy is to 'steer clear of controversy', suggests that Shiv should have stuck to only those facts which were pertinent to the lesson. According to him, those two facts are that Kalyana was a glorious Hindu kingdom and that Basava taught people the importance of uplifting the untouchables. Shiv is asked by the vice-chancellor of the university to retract the lesson, apologise and avoid media. Hariharan describes Shiv's life under siege with angst, combined with humour:

> Shiv sees his lesson sent to the corner in disgrace .... There is a warning sign that quarantines it from the other booklets, a sign like the ones on those ominously shaped vehicles. Caution! Highly Inflammable Medieval History. Only known antidotes: 500 mg of blissful ignorance or 250 mg of unadulterated lies. (86)

The story of Shiv is based on the real-life story of the playwright H.S. Shivaprakash to which Githa Hariharan refers to in the novel: "It seems there was a similar controversy in 1994. But that was about a play on Basava and the play was written in Kannada" (109). The play was published in 1986. It won a state award and was prescribed as a text book in a couple of universities. Eight years later, a similar group in Karnataka to which

Hariharan ironically calls, 'cousins, or ancestors of Shiv's Manch', accused the playwright of 'distorting' history and demanded the withdrawal of the play from the syllabus. Copies of the play were brunt and so was an effigy of the playwright. This became an election issue and finally 'in view of the law and order situation', the play was withdrawn in 1995 by the government order. Githa Hariharan reflects that today not only art but also history, which is a tool to understand both past and present, is under the same siege:

> Now, in 2000, the distance between the imaginary lands of literature and the prosaic city of history has shrunk. All occupy the same beleaguered space, the same territory under indefinite siege. The horizon, the sky, all wider-open spaces are reduced to the size of a pinpoint; the Manch and its cohorts are telling them all that there is only one way to remember a great man, *their* way. Only one way to remember the past. (110)

The novel shows how history is being used as "an armour, as propaganda, as battleground, as the seed of hatred" (132). In "New Voices, New Challenges", Githa Hariharan tells us that she has deliberately focused on history as these days history is quite a disputed area in India and is being used for the attainment of political ends with the result that, "the historical and cultural landmarks in people's minds have become disputed structures. Disputed sites" (*Littcrit*, 7).

The demolition of the Babri Masjid in 1992 was in fact a strategy to divide Hindus and Muslims through 'History' which resulted in communal riots and subsequently the Godhra massacre in Gujarat. "History", says Githa Hariharn in her interview with Gowri Ramanarayan, "is a tool to understand ourselves and our times. We may know that under a mosque there is a temple, but the problem begins when they come up with an 'authorised' official version of the past in its entirety, a whitewashed view of a single continuous, homogenous Hindu past, seeking a range of censorship rights" (*The Hindu*, April 24, 2003).

As a historian and professor, Shiv had made an attempt to disentangle the reality from the myth. What he had emphasised was that Basava was not "a cardboard saint singing syrup-sweet, devotional songs, only concerned with the hereafter" (104). He was a social reformer and a thinker who examined everything that was traditionally 'sanctioned'. He questioned the idea of 'the Hindu world' as being a homogeneous whole and protested against all kinds of discriminations. He gathered around him a number of social revolutionaries known as veerashaivas-warriors of Shiva and the movement came to be known as virasaiva movement. Together with them, he attempted to experiment with a community that 'sought to exclude no one', a community in which 'cross currents could co-exist', and in which 'rapids and the most placid of waters were fellow travellers' (107). The movement wrought a social upheaval and the city of Kalyana was ultimately burnt. But Basava and his companions left a legacy, a legacy Shiv is now heir to it but in a very different way. He would have liked to believe that it is Basava who links the year 1168 and 2000 but he is agonised to see that "it is not the dissident leader who is the critical link but the same hate mongers, the same manches that have sprouted in two times, centuries apart" (109).

Basava's passionate questions are relevant even today. But Shiv realises that "only a sanitised Basava is allowed to remain, a saint singer, a singer with a saintly face. This toothless man is safe enough to be hung on walls, a bland calendar memory" (86). As his ideas clash with the vested interests and make life uncomfortable the best way is to "turn a leader into a minor god: the man into saint that is the only way to make him safely untouchable Then his ideas and politics need not be understood" (92).

What Hariharan is emphasising here is how we short-change the collective memory of the great leaders by putting them on pedestals. K.V. Subanna, the Magsaysay award winner says, "Basavanna, a rebel himself, becomes an icon you cannot write about" (Deshpande, 2003: 230). Deshpande goes on to say in "The Enemy Within":

> A particular group decides it is the custodian of its own history, its myths, its leaders. It determines that their voice is the only voice that should be heard on these things; that their version is the right version; there can be no other and there can be no debate ... . More sinister is the fact of the governments giving in to these pressure groups ... the appeasement policy comes into play when the pressure group forms a large vote bank. (2003: 230)

Shiv is in the process of writing another lesson on the rise and fall of the Vijayanagar empire. He sees the Vijayanagar empire not just as 'a mighty Hindu Kingdom plundered by a Muslim foe' but also as a city "which reduced the subjects into subjection, a city where everything was intended to dwarf and diminished the individual citizen, grandeur invariably built on the blood and sweat of hovels swallowed up by time" (158). This is the picture that Shiv gathers on his field trip to Hampi and feels a great desire to "weed out stereotypes and reconstruct an entire range of possibilities, making realistic assessments" (40). He is reminded of his father who used to say that to get hold of something and learn all about it, what is required is free thinking. This inspires him but then his mind drifts to 'the looters of the past' who would accuse him of 'tainting' the glory of the model Hindu kingdom of Vijaynagar and also of 'under-playing' Muslim plundering of Vijaynagar empire. He knows that what is expected from him is to write that Vijaynagar was a glorious Hindu empire, a peak of the Hindu past and heritage and that the empire was defeated in a battle and the great city was looted by the Muslim kings. He is made to think if there is only one way to know ideas or people or the past. Githa Hariharan very sharply comments upon the shrinkage of space for free expression as a result of the polarisation of the society along caste and communal lines:

> History, its layered terrain of past merging into present, shrinks to the size of a module, a black and white booklet of lesson. Then that too goes. There is only a lone orphaned atom left behind, a sullen, impoverished particle of knowledge. The world and its multitudinous mysteries are reduced to precarious survival on a crude see saw: saint versus leader, saint versus man. Golden Age versus Dark Age. Hindu versus Muslim, Hindu versus Christian, anti Hindu, pro-Hindu. Secularist, pseudo Secularist, soft Hindu, rabid Hindu. (150)

Shiv feels his eloquence about the complexities of history "drying up at the thought of confronting fists, threats, physical danger in any form at all" (57) and asks himself "is it possible to write history-or anything else at all-if you have to worry about your masters, objections, their venal sentiments" (157). In this connection, Ramachandra Guha, a writer and historian says, "I want to write biographies of Ambedkar and of Golwalkar. But I cannot write about Ambedkar because I am not a Dalit and I cannot write about Golwalkar because I am not a fully paid-up member of the RSS (Anjali Puri, *Outlook*: 33). Meena, a young activist in the novel, asks Shiv Murthy, "How do we beat your fundoos at their game?" Shiv wonders that fundamentalism has become so much a fact of life that "a nick name 'fundoos' rolls off Meena's tongue with ease, a nick name for a pet, a pet enemy ... . Fundoo. fundamentalist. Fascist. Obscurantist. Terrorist. And the made-in-India brand, the communalist, a deceptively innocuous-sounding name for professional other-community haters" (57).

In the novel, there are other real-life stories taken from contemporary life which run parallel to the main narrative and further emphasise the insidious role of the communal forces. Amar, a young activist in the novel, recounts: "the murder of Australian missionary, Graham Staines and his two children ... the attacks on the artist M.F. Husain for painting Hindu goddess in the nude ... the recall of a volume on the freedom struggle and the disruption of the shooting of a film on the plight of Hindu widows in Benares." He concludes: "the list is endless" (100).

There was a time when the term slash and burn brought to mind a form of shifting cultivation practised from ancient times. In the past two decades with the ascendance of majoritarian politics in India, the term has exemplified a trajectory of political opportunism characterised by a virulent aesthetic of violence in public space—especially in the cultural terrain. For fifteen years the Hindutva campaign to isolate, target and brand the iconic artist M.F. Hussain as a deviant, connecting his 'crimes' with his community's 'disloyalty' has been a grim example of this form of political mobilisation. Hundreds of cases instituted against him across India for executing a 'nude' drawing of Saraswati have kept the artist in exile, uprooted from his cultural environment that has nourished his creativity. The irony is that India's premier art fair, the Indian Art Summit chose to ignore the artist whose name is synonymous with the creation of a market for Indian contemporary art, although in a defensive move—corrupting public space into an exclusionary, sanitised and monetised space.

Similarly, in February, 2000, Deepa Mehta was to direct the film 'Water' in India, the third in a trilogy. The first 'Fire' is a story of two middle-class women drawn together in search of the warmth that their loveless marriage lacked. The lesbian relationship between the women angered Shiv Sena activists and they went on a rampage against the film. They went to the extent of burning the cinema hall that first screened the film. The second film, 'Earth', was a love story encompassing conflicting religions and politics between India and Pakistan. The film 'Water' to which Githa Hariharan refers to in the novel is about the plight of widows in India. The story is located in the holy city of Varanasi, a place where homes for widows still exist. There is a building on the Ganges that was left in a will to shelter widows but the two top floors of this building have been converted into a restaurant and a guest house, while the lower floor, which is completely in a rundown condition, houses widows who are surviving by begging and who often turn to prostitution. The day before the shooting was scheduled, a mob led by three political/religious parties—BJP, Vishwa Hindu Parishad and Kashi Sanskrit Raksha Sangharsh Samiti—came forward with threats of violence against the director. The mob destroyed the main film set and burnt the effigies of Deepa Mehta. Most recently we have seen Shiv Sainiks attempts to stop the release of Shah Rukh Khan's film 'My Name is Khan' for his 'anti national statements'. Some months ago the Maharashtra Navnirman Samiti (MNS) successfully extracted an apology from the producer Karan Johar for the 'insult' caused to Marathi *manoos* in the film "Wake up Sid" by the mere mention of Mumbai as Bombay.

Hariharan also refers to the recalling of the volume on the freedom movement by K.N. Pannikar and Sumit Sarkar who became victims of 'the self-appointed cultural police' during the national democratic alliance regime because it was different from the version that they had wanted.

The references to these real-life stories in the novel bring into question the notion of public sphere in India as a democratic space encouraging a diversity of views or dissent against majoritarianism. "Openness to new ideas", observes Anjali Puri in *Outlook*, "and a willingness to discuss them rationally in the public domain seem to be alarmingly in short supply" (30). The injunctions spring from political parties, cultural outfits or religious organisations to ban or proscribe whenever there is a comment, film, book, or a play which gives a version other than what they want. In this connection, Shashi Deshpande writes:

> Increasing intolerance is being translated into a concern for what is called 'our culture', which leads a particular group into becoming sensitive about a particular issue, giving it a chance to show its muscle, clout and its political power. (2003: 230)

In her essay "New Voices, New Challenge" included in *Littcrit*, Githa Hariharan tells the reader that she has deliberately set the novel in a university to emphasise that the process of learning is supposed to break down walls and enlarge the student's world rather than shrink it by feeding it with prejudices. If a free and frank debate is discouraged in a university set up, this shows the insidious role of communal forces.

Shiv, otherwise a quiet man, takes a bold step when the Manch retaliates violently to the protest rallies and demonstrations organised by the left-wing university students and destroys his office damaging it considerably . He tells the Dean that he will not apologise to the Manch. In an interview with Kala Krishnan Ramesh, Githa Hariharan says:

> It is not just Shiv of the novel, but all the decent, respectable, middle class people like Shiv are required to come out and say that they need these basic freedoms as the mildest sort of tolerance of any bigotry or chauvinism will bite like the cobra in the pitcher if you put your hand in. (*The Hindu*, April 24, 2003)

Of course, there is still no knowing if charring of canvases, vandalising of artistic spaces and institutions of excellence, disrupting of film and theatre performances or targeting of individual artistes will be dealt with similarly at the level of governance or political engagement.

'Fatwas' are also among the most visible culture cops and are feeding nothing but bigotry. This aspect of the present day reality is brought out by Githa Hariharan in one of her stories. The story is embedded in *When Dreams Travel*. It is reminiscent of the controversy over Salman Rushdie's book *The Satanic Verses* which unleashed a worldwide violence from Islamic fundamentalist organisations causing riots in which several people were killed. Governments throughout the Muslim world banned the book. Five months after the book was released, Ayatollah Khomeini, Iran's religious and political leader issued a 'fatwa' against the author condemning him to death. Rushdie went into hiding and remained in fearful seclusion for six years.

The narrative in *When Dreams Travel* combines fantasy and magic with satire and illustrates the perils that even the most acclaimed of writers like Salman Rushdie may encounter in an era of religious polarisation. Githa Hariharan has created a character called Satyasama who is a poet and has conveyed the story of controversy over *The Satanic Verses* through her story. The story is multi-dimensional. It also warns that if religious divide is encouraged, a multi-religious country like India will always remain on fire. Hariharan tells us why she has deliberately named the character 'Satyasama':

> Satyasama is necessary in our times of different fatwas; it's not just the Ayatollash's fatwa but our own day-to-day fatwas that you have all over the world. So that was necessary. Satyasama was also necessary because I wanted to have a link to India. I had to create a character who would-and even her name 'Satya' is from Sanskrit and it means 'truth' and 'Sama' is from the Arabic and it means 'the sky'—show the fact that actually our heritage is like this. I did want to combine Hindu and Islamic strands as it is experienced in day-to-day life in India. Nobody

> tells you that this strand of what you know is Hindu in origin. This is it: it all comes to you mixed up. It was this subtext as well ... I was looking at. (2004: 385)

The word 'Satyasama' assimilates and celebrates the composite culture of India which has been influenced by Vedas and Vedanta philosophy as well as by the Bhakti saints like Khusro and Kabir who taught that Ram and Rahim, Ishwar and Allah are the names of the same God. Like Satyasama of the story, who sang of 'storms; of changes in the sky', Salman Rushdie also warned in *The Satanic Verses* against the dangers of religious polarisation. In fact, he has often expressed his opposition to the religious extremism. The book also celebrates the intermingling of cultures, to use the words of Hariharan in the novel, "of clouds that drifted and rained whether they were in the east or west ... of the eternal marriage between east and west" (144) and attempts to establish a middle ground between eastern and western chauvinisms. But just as Satyasama in the story was suspected to be 'pro-westwalla and anti-eastwalla', Salman Rushdie was identified with the west. Hariharan ironically calls the fundamentalists the 'Eternals' and writes that they forbade Satyasama to sing her 'songs' but she refused. "Goaded by her unreasonable refusal, her tormentors locked her up in an underground chamber just enough air to keep her alive. ... A year later the department heads, in a merciful mood, reconsidered her case and she was brought up into the glare of day again" (147). Here Hariharan is alluding to how Salman Rushdie was forced to remain underground and the subsequent announcement by the Iranian president declaring the Rushdie affair over. In the novel, Githa Hariharan describes eastern and western chauvinism ironically:

> One of the symptoms of this madness was the growing belief (first secret, then not-so-secret) that the sky was not big enough for both sunrise and sunset. The sky divided Eternal

> City into the eastwallas and the westwallas. The easties felt their pupils dilate, gain sharpness and power and peace from the ascending light at sunrise. They worshipped that piece of eastern sky; chanted ten thousand and one names in its praise. They invariably greeted each other with the pious wish: 'May the light rise in the east tomorrow!' The westies found this early morning devotion a bizarre and alien thing. Surely anyone with an iota of sense for piety or love for motherland would see that it was the west he should turn to? (140–41)

Unfortunately, writes Hariharan, the world is divided not by "flowing rivers or craggy mountains that help us to cross the barriers they put up" (140) but by the growing differences among the people.

Githa Hariharan concludes the story of Satyasama, which runs parallel to that of Salman Rushdie, by saying that though she came out of the underground chamber there was a condition. The condition was that she was to give up her singing forever but she continued to sing and resisted to 'succumbing to the relief of silence' as long as she was alive. Salman Rushdie also continued to write even while in hiding and won Britain's prestigious Whitbread Award for the best novel of 1995 for *The Moor's Last Sigh*.

Deshpande's *Small Remedies* also lays bare the disturbing truths of sectarian destructiveness and strife. But while Hariharan in *In Times of Siege* looks at the events with an almost photographically realistic lens, in Deshpande's works the actual incidents are not directly narrated She exposes the innermost psychological consequences of communal hate, of violence, of death and looks indirectly and inwardly through protagonist Madhu whose son is killed in a bomb explosion in a bus during the Bombay riots. Stricken by overwhelming grief, Madhu does not want to live any more but then she thinks she has to continue with life to find out the reasons behind such incidents.

She struggles to understand how far removed events can so easily snatch away the certainties that people have taken for granted. Bombay riots remind her of the riots in the year 1947–48 but she can see the difference between the two. This time there is a sense of "an efficient malignant force at work, working out its plans through mobs. Even people living in safe middle-class apartments way above the ground, can feel the subterranean rumblings" (229). 'Hostility, suspense and anger' have become a part of life and there is a 'miasma, the smell of the disaster in the air'.

In "Postcoloniality after 1947: The Split Identity of the Nation", Veena Singh points out how the concepts of the 'self' and the 'other' have changed. Before the Independence if there was any 'other', it was the British—the coloniser. But with the declaration of the Independence the attention from the 'outsider' shifted to 'home' (2004: 290). Madhu's resolve to take revenge culminates into an understanding that violence is induced into public life by the power—mongers.: "whose eyes do I exact in revenge? Which one human in the faceless mob can I hold responsible? And what do you do when the masks of evil are taken off and you see instead the faces of vulnerable human beings" (122–23). Through the narrative of Madhu, Deshpande highlights how the innocent people become victims of religious intolerance which changes the course of their lives. The novel portrays with remarkable precision the web of human connections that binds as well as divides. There are people like Hamidbhai, Tony and Joe who have been very kind and generous to her. Even Ghulam Saab's daughter is accepted, though not easily, as Shailaja Joshi. The novel also shows communal forces at work. Hasina, Ghulam Saab's grand daughter, is to give an all-night performance at the Bhawani temple. She receives threats that she would not be allowed to sing in the temple. Madhu, dressed in salwar kameez is mistaken for Hasina and is attacked to send out the message that Hasina cannot sing in the temple. Ravi, who is making arrangements for the performance, is persuaded by the police to change the programme. But he is determined that he will not allow a public performance to be converted into 'a small closed room' conflict between religions and knows that it is "the work of outsiders ... of politicians who are trying to extract some advantage for themselves out of this. The elections are in a few months ..." (296). Hasina, on the other hand, is scared, "My parents live in Bombay, my mother was so shocked after the riots, she fell ill. It is always the innocent who suffer, I don't want anyone to die, I don't want people to suffer because of me" (297). The novel shows the vulnerability of the individual in the face of fundamentalism. But, at the same time, Shashi Deshpande stresses the need to resist. Hasina, does sing in the temple finally. The novel, as Meenakshi Mukherjee says, "takes in one large sweep the plurality, diversity and at the same time the contradictions of our contemporary culture" (2004: 175).

There are other real-life stories embedded in other works of Shashi Deshpande. The story of Kalpana in *The Binding Vine*, a young girl who is raped brutally, is based on the real-life story of a nurse in Bombay. Shashi Deshpande acknowledges this in her conversation with Lakshmi Holmstrom:

> The theme came to me very suddenly. I was actually working on another novel, and one day, suddenly I realised that this was what I had to write. It started with an accident that happened in a hospital when my husband was working there. We were staying next to the nurses' quarters at the time. There was a particular nurse whom we used to see everyday coming and going. A very pretty, attractive woman, a radiant kind of person. She was raped, she was found unconscious in the basement of one of the hospital buildings and she never recovered consciousness. It is seventeen years now, and she is still alive. (1998: 249–50)

Kalpana's mother Shakutai, who is a working woman, demands a silence, a repression of the truth for she is afraid that it will bring disgrace to Kalpana and will also adversely affect the chances of marriage for her younger daughter:

> If a girl's honour is lost, what is left? The girl doesn't have to do anything wrong ... people will themselves point a finger at her ... even if it is true, keep it to yourself, don't let anyone know of it. I have another daughter, what will become of her ...? (59)

The opprobrium that the matter will attract is more terrifying to Kalpana's mother than the desire to find the culprit and punish him. "This exposes", as Vijaya Guttal points out in "*The Binding Vine* and *A Matter of Time*: A Reading in the Postcolonial Context", "the society's attitude towards the rape victim and the patriarchal ideology that rape disgraces the victim rather than the culprit" (2005: 172). Moreover, Shakutai, holds her daughter responsible for all that has happened to her. Kalpana was very fond of being dressed up like other girls of her age, using lipstick and nail-paint. Her mother, who has internalised patriarchal ideology, kept her telling, 'Cover yourself decently ... . But she went her way. You should have seen her walking out, head in the air, caring for no body. Its all her fault ... all her fault' (147). Kalpana had to pay a heavy price for transgressing the boundaries within which she was expected to confine herself. The Police also insist on repressing the truth because rape cases are 'messy and troublesome, never straightforward'(88). Not only that, they also believe that '... she must have been out with a boyfriend ... May be after they had a bit of fun she was knocked down by a car' (88). The doctor who tells the media what really happened is pressurised by the officials not to give his report and receives the threat of dismissal.

The situation becomes worse when the case is turned into a matter of consent. There is also an article by a 'sociologist' in the newspaper saying that "there can be no rape, because it can't be done unless the woman is willing" and also an article by a poet who wants "to forgive the rapist for he knows not what he is doing" (182). The role of the media is also baffling. One of the newspapers in Marathi writes 'ek Kalpanechi Katha' (a concocted story), punning on Kalpana's name and other newspapers glorify the case by calling her parents martyrs. The issue becomes a game in which charges and counter charges are exchanged.

Kalpana's story reflects the real-life story of Mathura also, a sixteen year old tribal girl from Chandrapur district, Maharashtra. She was taken to the police station by her brother and other relatives as she was under age and yet was attempting to elope with her lover. The two policemen on duty said that they wanted to record Mathura's statement in private. They raped her while her relatives waited outside. The Session Judge held that since she had earlier eloped with her boyfriend, she must have been habituated to sex and could not be raped. The High Court reversed the judgment sentencing the policemen to six years in prison. In 1979, the Supreme Court again reversed the order. The judges felt that since Mathura had not raised any alarm and since there were no visible injury marks on her body, she must have given her consent.

The Mathura rape case stimulated the women's movement into asking for reforms of the criminal law that dealt with rape. In 1983 the government passed the Criminal Law Amendment Act. These amendments were not enough to stem the rise in the number of cases of sexual violence against women. Based on the Law Commission's recommendations, the government enacted an amendment in 2002 which provided that a victim of rape can no longer be questioned about her past sexual conduct and her 'general immoral character'. Despite the Sexual Assault Bill, several cases of rape continue to be reported.

Another story in the novel, which runs parallel to the story of Kalpana, is the story of Mira. Though Mira is a married woman, Urmila, the protagonist realises that "what has happened to Kalpana happened to Mira too" (63). This is a story of rape within marriage and in this way the two stories come together.

Mira is Urmila's mother-in-law who dies after giving birth to Kishore, Urmila's husband. Urmila learns from Akka, Kishore's foster mother married to Mira's bereaved husband, about her husband's obsession with Mira, his single minded object to marry her after he had seen at a wedding ceremony. Significantly, a trunk of Mira, that has long been sealed, is given to Urmila. In the trunk Urmi finds diaries and poems which Mira has written. As she goes through them, she finds that through all her writing runs 'an intense dislike of the sexual act with her husband, a kind of physical repulsion from the man she married ... did it have its genesis ... during their first night together?' (63). Urmi reads in a diary entry her hatred for the very word 'love' as it amounts to sex against her desire:

> Love! How I hate the word. If this is love, it is a terrible thing. I have learnt to say 'no' at last, but it makes no difference, no difference at all. What is it he wants from me? I look at myself in the mirror and wonder, what is there in me? Why does it have to be me? Why can't he leave me alone? (67)

Urmi realises that Mira's husband tried to 'possess another human being against her will' (83). In "Survivors: Changing attitudes to Divorce among Women", Jaisingh Indrani, an eminent lawyer writes:

> It is assumed that by marrying a man, a woman has given her consent to sexual intercourse with her husband any time. Thus, even if he forces himself on her, he is not committing an offence (of rape) as her consent is assumed. In this respect, the

women's movement has consistently demanded that the law of rape be changed. (1993: 65)

Mira's story, as Jasbir Jain points out in *Gendered Realities, Human Spaces: The Writing of Shashi Deshpande*, reflects the real-life story of Rukhmabai of the 1880s which raised several questions regarding a woman's right to her body and her willingness or otherwise to enter into a relationship. Rukhmabai was born in Bombay in 1864 and was married to Dadaji Bhikaji when she was just eleven years old, her husband nineteen. But she did not live with him and remained with her mother and stepfather. In 1884 a long battle between Rukhmabai and Dadaji began, when he asserted his right in the court and wanted her to live with him. She got an initial victory when the court maintained that restitution could not be claimed where no conjugal relations had taken place. But the second hearing went in favour of her husband and she was ordered by the court to stay with her husband or face a prison sentence. Rukhmabai told the court that she would willingly suffer imprisonment rather than join her husband. Her defiance became a public issue and led to the need of reshaping Indian society where individuals, ideas and institutions are interlocked in complex relationships of compromise and antagonism.

Stories of Mira and Kalpana bring into question a woman's right to her body. In the novel, there is a reference to a case filed by a husband against his wife on the restitution of conjugal rights. Priti, a young star in the novel is excited that the judgement went in favour of the wife that she could not be forced into a sexual relationship with the husband against her will. But then Urmi retorts that one judgement by a single judge can be appealed against and overruled. Shashi Deshpande contends that laws have to be accompanied by a much wider range of actions to tackle patriarchal institutions.

We can see that in the works of both Shashi Deshpande and Githa Hariharan the main story may be about one individual but they transcend the boundaries of personal narrative. Several real-life stories, included and referred to, both from history and contemporary life, make their works at once sociological treatises, historical and political records, feminist critiques. The real-life stories also show the concern and sensitivity of these two writers who have examined some of the major social issues through their writings.

References

Deshpande, Shashi. "Of Concerns, Of Anxieties", *Women in Indo Anglian Fiction: Tradition and Modernity*. Ed. Naresh K. Jain. New Delhi: Manohar Publications, 1998.

——. "Writing and Activism", *Writing Difference: Novels of Shashi Deshpande*. Ed. Chanchala K. Naik. New Delhi: Pencraft International, 2005.

——. "Shashi Deshpande Talks to Lakshmi, Holmstrom", *The Fiction of Shashi Deshpande*. Ed. R.S. Pathak. New Delhi: Creative Books, 1998.

Guttal, Vijaya. "*The Binding Vine* and *A Matter of Time*: A Reading in the Postcolonial Context", *Writing Difference: The Novels of Shashi Deshpande*. Ed. Chanchala K. Naik. New Delhi: Pencraft International, 2005.

Hariharan, Githa. "Close to the Bone", an interview with Kala Krishnan Ramesh. *The Hindu*, 24 April, 2003.

——. "New Voices: New Challenges". *Littcrit*, Vol. 30, No. 1, June 2004.

——. "Discreet Thoughts", *Desert in Bloom: Contemporary Indian Women's Fiction in English*. Ed. Meenakshi Bharat. Delhi: Pencraft International, 2004.

——. "Plea for Pluralism", an interview with Gowri Ramanarayan. *The Hindu*, 24 April, 2003.

——. "How I Write and Why? Githa Hariharan Answers", *Of Narratives, Narrators*. Eds. Rajul Bhargava and Shubhshree. Jaipur and New Delhi: Rawat Publications, 2004.

Indrani, Jaisingh. "Survivors: Changing Attitudes to Divorce among Women", *Uncertain Laisons*. Eds. Khushwant Singh and Shobha De. New Delhi: Penguin India, 1993.

Jain, Jasbir. *Gendered Realities, Human Spaces: The Writing of Shashi Deshpande*. New Delhi: Pencraft International, 2003.

Lakshman, Nirmala. "Address at 'A Meet-the-Author Event'". <http://www.githahariharn.com/htm. 15/9/07.

Mukherjee, Meenakshi. "On Her Own Terms: A Reading of Shashi Deshpande's *Small Remedies*", *Desert in Bloom: Contemporary Indian Women's Fiction in English*. Ed. Meenakshi Bharat. Delhi: Pencraft International, 2004.

Puri, Anjali. "Shush: Boo". *Outlook*, December 12, 2005.

Rushdie's *Satanic Verses*. www.indiastar.com/jsamuel.html-24k http://sify.com/printer_friendly.php?id=14203722&ctid=2&lid =1. 13 May, 2006.

Singh, Veena. "Postcoloniality after 1947: The Split Identity of the Nation", *Contesting Postcolonialisms*. Eds. Jasbir Jain and Veena Singh. Jaipur and Delhi: Rawat Publications, 2004.

CHAPTER 4

Stories of Survival

'Survival' is a major preoccupation with both Shashi Deshpande and Githa Hariharan. Their protagonists suffering from loneliness, dilemmas and frustrations, make an attempt towards a better understanding of themselves and the world around them. As they explore the complexities of life they are confronted with, it often leads them to a search for strategies of survival. There is a striving on their part towards arriving at a more authentic way of life than the one which is available to them and in this process they discover the latent possibilities of life. The main urge always is to survive. For instance, Mira in *The Binding Vine* is overwhelmed by a sense of the utter futility of living, yet she is "terrified by the thought of dying, of ceasing to be" (203). She takes to writing "that kept her going, that kept her alive" (127). This writing also creates an imaginative space for her. So it is not just physical survival but the struggle for self-expression and self-realisation which is evident in all their writings. As it is beset with all manner of complexities, they consistently problematise it and invariably connect the issue with gender considerations which often calls into question various social structures, practices and customs.

Each individual has a 'self' which is different from that of the others and the loss of this 'self' will be the loss of his/her identity. The realisation of this 'self' is the realisation of one's potentialities and the strength of a human being lies in the attainment of this 'selfhood'. *The Dark Holds No Terrors* begins by saying "You are your own refuge, there is no other refuge. This refuge is hard to achieve." Shashi Deshpande here, as Usha Bande points out, "seems to suggest that there is no easy solution to life's existential problems" (2005: 191). An urge to compete, to excel, to defeat and to survive is a part of human nature and equally basic is the urge to love, share, communicate and relate to others. Moreover, one finds that such communication and involvement with others are necessary not only for survival, but also for full realisation of one's potential. One strives for the expression of both these urges in one's social life. The two have to be harmonised. Yet all efforts at maintaining the balance often fail. This is one more perpetual challenge that one has to face. Various social institutions, structures and mechanism have been devised to achieve this end but they themselves impose constraints. In her conversation with June Gaur, Shashi Deshpande says:

> The family is a timeless and universal institution—everything begins here, everything that happens outside the family mirrors what happens within it. I have always been fascinated by human relationships; the locale within which the relationships are looked at is immaterial. In fact, relationships in families are most intense and most complex. To speak of the

> family's 'domestic scope'—how cozy the word 'domestic' is and how uncozy the things that happen in families are … . (*The Hindu*, September 5, 2004)

No matter how necessary or supportive family structures may be, they reduce personal space. This is a contradiction that cannot be fully resolved. There is this constant struggle between one's urge for survival and self-expression and one's awareness of oneself in relation to multiple other selves. In almost all her novels, Shashi Deshpande shows a concern with families and space. Sarita in *Dark Holds No Terrors* realises: "if I caste no shadow, I do not exist", but at the same time she also knows that "all those selves she had rejected ... the guilty sister, the undutiful daughter, the unloving wife ... she had to accept these selves to become whole again" (220).

Through her female characters, Shashi Deshpande calls into question the very notion of freedom. The idea of 'independence' and notions of 'freedom' are never what they seem, whether male or female. The term 'autonomy' carries with it the idea of the right of all individuals to make choices freely and independently. But as an individual is a social and cultural product, he is, to quote Stuart Hall, "always lodged and implicated in the practices and structures of everybody else's life" and therefore cannot be totally free (2003: 229). In one's urge for survival and self-realisation, one has to combat with forces—both contingent and incidental. It is very difficult to be 'independent' or 'free of history'.

This is true that an individual is constrained by and is free only within the circumstances of a given history, yet both Shashi Deshpande and Githa Hariharan believe that within those circumstances, individual choices can be exercised and they can make history. They seem to agree with Sartre who, though he believed that 'existence precedes essence', defined man in terms of his commitment and always saw a choice in the situation. The true existential being surfaces only when one chooses authentically even when faced with conflicting values. "To achieve anything, you have got to be hard and ruthless". This is how Shashi Deshpande's *That Long Silence* begins. When asked in an interview by Geetha Gangadharan if, as a woman or as an individual, she subscribes to this philosophy, Shashi Deshpande answers:

> Yes, very much so. Unless you are ruthless, you really can't achieve much in life. Take any achiever and you see that the ladders are usually made up of other people. It takes a very hard person to do that but there are people who have done that. The lack of women achievers is because of our incapability to be ruthless. Women are more sensitive and do not give up on individual needs and pulls easily. It is more important for us to be loved and liked as individuals with the family. (1998: 254)

Shashi Deshpande's *Small Remedies* is, to quote Usha Bande, "the story of all those who defy, suffer, endure and yet stand up to face life ... a profound piece of writing about love and loss, grief and hope, rebellion and sacrifice and above all about the Promethean will to resist, endure and survive" (2005: 198–199). In the main text, there are two parallel narratives of two women, Leela and Savitribai. Both the women stepped out of their straitjacketed roles, exercised their options as individuals, pursued their dreams and realised them. Leela devoted the whole of her life to the cause of the society despite of the criticism that she faced and Savitribai pursued music with a similar single mindedness .

The story unfolds in the small town of Bhavanipur where Savitribai Indorekar, a well-known classical singer has settled in the last days of her life. Madhu, the protagonist and the narrator arrives there, apparently to interview Savitribai in order to write her biography, but in actuality she has taken up this assignment to escape from the reminders of the tragic death of her only son, Aditya. But Madhu's own story is incomplete without the presence of an equally powerful character Leela; her aunt. What makes the book both interesting and complex is the way the main story turns out to be not just Madhu's or Savitribai's, but also that of Leela's.

Savitribai's story of success comes to us with its accompanying angst as the novel goes on to reflect the history of that time. Born in an affluent Brahmin family she shared with her mother a love of music. Tutored by her mother, who used to sing 'aarti', 'ritual songs' and 'stotras', the child sang at a family gathering. But before she could complete the song, she was silenced by her grand mother.

Savitribai was not allowed to sing or learn music by her father and grand-parents as they did not want her "to be one of *those* women?" (62). Music at that time was associated with those professional women who were kept outside the circle of the 'respectable' society. It is, as Jasbir Jain has stated, "this notion of 'respectability' that confines a woman's talents and demands a heavy sacrifice from her" (2003: 255). It was in her father-in-law's house that Savitribai seized the opportunity to start on music. Her father-in-law was very fond of music. Though he himself could not become an expert singer, he patronised musicians and arranged performances for them both in his own house and outside. There were two rooms in her father-in-laws' house, separated from the rest of the house and the doors of those rooms were always locked. It was there that the musicians stayed. It was a 'forbidden' world for women. Though her father-in-law was liberal and believed in girls' education, there was a clear dividing line between what females could do and what they could not. "Associating with musicians definitely lay outside the Laxman Rekha" (218).

There was a window opening into the corridor through which one could hear the music. Savitribai could not resist the temptation and thought that if she sat under the window, she would be invisible and in this way she could listen to the musicians. One day her father-in-law, passing along the corridor, saw the open window. As he was going to shut it, he saw Savitribai crouching on the floor. She was terrified but he said nothing and moved on, leaving the window open the way it had been. He not only let it go but also sent a message that there was to be a performance and the women could listen to it if they wanted to. The door would be open but they would have to stay on the 'other' side of the house.

This practice of keeping the women 'on the other side of the house', 'antahpura' or the 'zanana' was with a purpose—to deny any public space to women and to limit them to their domestic roles. Savitribai could no longer pretend that 'the mundane domestic' life that she was leading satisfied her. She took a bold step. She went into his room with and left a note pleading to be allowed to learn music and she is allowed both lessons and an opportunity to attend concerts. It was really a revolutionary step on the part of her father-in-law to allow his daughter-in-law to learn music. Shashi Deshpande comments ironically on the social system when she writes:

> For a man, a wealthy man and the head of the family, to indulge in his love of music, even to have a singer as a mistress, was all right. But for a daughter-in-law to be learning music, and that seriously, as if she was going to be a professional. Surely there was outrage, surely there was anger in the family. Rules could be modified for the daughters, sometimes they were, purely out of affection, but daughters-in-law carry the weight of the honour of the family, its reputation, its *Izzat*. (220)

Jasbir Jain in "Cultural Rooting/Routing through English" points out that "languages do not develop in a vacuum; they are rooted in a cultural context and words evoke certain responses" (2005: 35). Words like 'honour', 'dishonour', 'right', 'wrong', when put in the context of men's lives, they mean something different but when put in the context of women's lives, they seek to define and limit her. 'Izzat', and 'Lazza' are particularly used in the context of a woman's life to limit her. Shashi Deshpande also in "Telling Our Own Stories" points out that 'words and ideas do not mean the same to women as they mean to men because the meanings of words have been built around the interests of men, the reason being that women have not participated in the process of word-making' (2003: 96). In *A Matter of Time* Sumi wonders whether it was 'honour' that forced Dashratha to fulfill the promise he had made years back and send Ram into exile. But was this 'honour' worth all the tragedy that followed. She also questions if Kaushalya would have sent her son into exile to keep the honour of a promise made years back (157). Similarly, in "The Inner Rooms" also, Amba questions 'the meaningless rigmarole of words' and says that words like 'honour', 'dishonour', 'right', 'wrong' have been used by men to cover their real emotions.

Though, in a way, Savitribai had her father-in-law's support and encouragement Madhu could imagine that it must have taken enormous courage on her part to face the 'anger, derision, contempt, ridicule ... the jibes and the hostility' of other women when she came out of her music room:

> To be set apart from your own kind, not to be able to conform, to flout the rules laid down, is to lay yourself open to cruelty. Animals know this, they do it more openly, their cruelty towards the deviant is never concealed. But the subtle cruelty of persistent hostility leaves deeper wounds. (220–221)

While relating her story, Savitribai never mentioned any of the hardships that she had faced. Her silence "glosses over both her struggle and her endurance" (221). Only once she gave voice to her feelings "sometimes I wished that I had been born in one of those musicians' families in which I would naturally have become a singer. In those families, you are born into the profession. There is never any problem even for women" (221). But even those women, writes Shashi Deshpande, who were born in professional families, remained 'outside the circle of respectable society'. Because of their birth, they were denied the life of ordinary woman. If they had the 'freedom' to be artistes, they were denied the right to live like the most women do. The inherent difficulties of living a life that satisfies the creative desire in a woman is brought out by Jasbir Jain:

> Savitribai's case illustrates with great realism the truth of with Virginia Woolf has expressed in *A Room of One's Own*. There are not so many female artists primarily because women have never had the same space or opportunity. In India, performing arts have always been a problematic profession for women, at least till a couple of decades ago, before the onslaught of electronic media … . The choice before Savitribai was clear, it had to be one or the other. There was simply no question of combining the two. (2003: 118)

There is always a temptation to take the 'normal' path and be accepted. But Bai did not succumb to this temptation. Her search for a good teacher is another long story of struggle. The lady-teacher that her father-in-law arranged for her was not good but she helped Savitribai by getting permission to introduce a tabla player into her classes. This was a turning point in Savitribai's life. It was at this time that she left her in –laws' house and came to live in Bombay with Ghulam Sahab, the tabla player, in search of her guru Kashinath Buwa. She first heard him during a Ganpati festival in Bombay at the home of a family friend when she was still living with her in-laws. She expressed her desire to be his disciple but he dismissed the idea because he thought music was no profession for a respectable married woman. She could take up music as a hobby and not as a profession and for that "there were others who could teach her" (130). But Bai did not give up. Once in Bombay, she went to him almost every other day, trying to persuade him but he was adamant. She was disappointed when he fell ill. But he recovered and left Bombay for Bhawanipur, his home town to live the rest of his life near the Bhawani temple. She followed him and told him that she would not leave Bhawanipur and would sit outside his house without food or drink until he agreed to take her as his pupil. He finally agreed but he did not give in totally and laid down his own conditions. She agreed to everything but regretted the only fact that she could not live near the temple like other male students who had the advantage of listening to him doing 'Riaz' and also the benefit of the classes he suddenly decided to take. For Savitribai, it became a curse a woman and more so a Brahmin woman belonging to a respectable family.

Savitribai's story is a sad comment on the social structure which goes on to privilege one over the other. Kabir and Eklavya were reprimanded by their 'gurus' because they came from the lower strata of society. Savitribai was penalised because she was a woman from a respectable Brahmin family.

Savitribai had to go through a lot of physical hardships. She had to travel by the local shuttle train to get to guruji's place with a two mile walk through the fields. The house in which she lived was also in very bad condition. There were just two rooms with a toilet outside, shared by others. There was no electricity and water had to be drawn from the well. Madhu wonders at the enormous courage shown by her:

> A young woman who had lived the sheltered life of the daughter-in-law of an affluent Brahmin family, living this kind of life.

> A woman who had been, both as a child and as a married girl, part of a large family, living in a strange town among total strangers. With the added burden of being a Hindu woman, a married Hindu woman ... (38)

As Madhu explores Savitribai's life, she finds that Savitribai has defied all cultural assumptions. She steps across the threshold and breaks out of the restrictions of upper caste patriarchal society in search of her dream. In her conversation with Madhu, she does not at all mention her daughter Munni, who is Madhu's childhood friend and who is later killed in a bomb blast, nor does she make any recognition of Madhu. Madhu, whom motherhood has absorbed to the extent of self-denial, wonders:

> In this story I see the artist, the woman in search of her genius, of her destiny. But the artist was born out of the woman. First there was the woman and then the artist. Is it possible to cut the umbilical cord, to sever the connection between the two? Did Bai manage to do this? (133)

Madhu tries to probe into whether it was Bai who disowned Munni or it was Munni who disowned her mother and gets confused. Here the comments made by Anne Collette are very relevant:

> Bai has gained the title of Savitribai Indorekar, Doyen Hindustani music (28)—but it is a title and the achievement of a dream won only in battle against the terrible weapons of a social orthodoxy that defines the parameters of a life in terms of class/caste and gender, and patrols those borders relentlessly. Victory in such a battle is won at no small cost, and in Bai's case it would appear to be won only through the denial of motherhood (whether that denial be of her daughter's choosing or her own is of little matter). (2004: 74)

Savitribai's forgetfulness regarding her daughter is deliberate and this is perhaps, as Jasbir Jain has also stated, "the struggle that has exacted its price and brought about the hardening of emotions, a kind of ruthlessness that Shashi Deshpande sees as an essential basis for survival" (2003: 222). Madhu also comes to realise that Bai is much more than Munni's mother:

> Now, after all these sessions with Bai, I know that Bai looks back at the young woman training under her guruji, the young woman living in one room and travelling between it and guruji's home, as her truest self. Free for the first time in years, living the life she wanted, steady in the pursuit of her goal, pure of purpose. (170)

Deshpande gives many examples which reveal that many of the hardships that Bai endured were due to her gender. In Neemgoan, where each family had been marked out according to religion, caste, money etc., the families of both Savitribai and Madhu were radically different from the other families. Savitribai lived with a Muslim and Madhu's father, who was a widower, brought up her daughter on his own with only a male servant at home. He never observed festivals and pujas. Moreover, he 'drank'. Still he was accepted with all his 'peculiarities and foibles', whereas Savitribai, who was called 'the singer woman' with something derogatory meaning attached to the word. Her performances "were permitted, possibly tolerated, but it did not take away the aura of disapproval" (139). Simone De Beauvoir in *The Second Sex* pointed out that women were constrained by the social roles and as such could not exercise their existential freedom. She emphasised that unless women break away from their status as 'secondary', they would not be able to realise their human potential. Savitribai's struggle for freedom and self expression is a challenge to patriarchy, "not confronting it headlong but in discovering one's own strength as a woman" (Naik, 2005: 222). Speaking of Shashi Despande's *A Matter of Time* and *Small Remedies* Usha Bande writes:

> To contend that Shashi Deshpande concerns herself in these novels with female resistance would be to put the novels in a slot, to view them from a narrow angle and to insist upon the obvious. Deshpande is too subtle an artist to deal with the surfaces ... . Savitri Indorekar's rebellious act to break away from her family, for her love of music is not an isolated, whimsical individual decision. It transcends personal borders and becomes a part of the key social and political agendas undertaken by the late nineteenth century women such as Pandita Rama Bai, Anandi Bai Joshi, Kashi Bai Kanitkar, Tara Bai Shinde and others who had the courage to stand up against the oppressive social system. (2005: 193)

Another character in the same novel, which enters into public life despite of social barriers, is Leela. At the time when the remarriage of a widow was out of question, she remarried and that too a Christian. Before marriage her name was Sindhu. She was disowned by the family and became a figure little girls were threatened with when they were disobedient: "Do you want to become a Sindhu? ... The black sheep of the family. A widow who remarried and what was worse, infinitely worse, married a Christian man" (45). Leela taught for many years and worked among the factory workers. She also participated in the Quit India Movement and Anti-Price Rise Movement and did daring things during the emergency but her family members did not mention any of her achievements. In this context, Chanchala K. Naik observes:

> In almost all societies, a woman is culturally assigned norms of behaviour in which standards of conduct, taste and decorum

> set the boundaries for her as external signs of what it means to be seemingly proper and respectable within the differentiated hierarchy called gender. Any form of deviation from prescribed norms or any display of transgressive potential in violation to the ideal image of womanhood makes her an unruly woman to be ostracised by society. (2005: 224)

But Leela "resolute of purpose, straight and direct in all that she did in her life" pursued her goal and endured the barriers erected by the society" (225). She was a woman who had always supported herself. When her first husband Vasant died, she took up a job and educated her brother-in-law. Even after marrying Joe, who was a doctor with a fairly good income, she continued to live on her own money and continued to wear cotton sarees from the mills where her first husband had worked. After the death of Joe, she moved back into her Maruti Chawl home the very next day, the place where she had begun her married life at the age of fifteen. She participated in various social and political movements and worked as a leader of trade unions. She also worked in the crowded chawls among the cotton mills, worked for women who ignored their symptoms of TB and sent them to the clinic especially established for TB patients. She was also an active member of the Communist Party. In addition to all this, she was also a woman who was wholly supportive and loving in her role as a wife and surrogate mother. She successfully combined her personal and public life. It was Leela who brought motherless Madhu out of the terrifying vacuum she faced when her father had died. Leela married Joe, a man from another religion, with whom she shared neither food nor language. She could speak no English and knew nothing of literature or music—'the two great forces in Joe's life'. Still they built a lovely relationship, giving enough space to each other. Though she was kept out of Joe's family by Paula's (Joe's daughter by his first wife) atrocious behaviour, she still forged a relationship with each of them.

Leela was full of courage. When Joe died, she showed no outward expressions of grief though "something has gone out of her-a passion, a force, a fire" (149). A bit of this courage reappeared when workers were arrested during a railway strike and their families were thrown out of their homes. It was at this time that Indira Gandhi declared the emergency. She resisted it. Though she was in a frail condition, she involved herself with the workers and their families, seeking justice for them. She did many daring things and remained in prison for nearly a year. In her last days, Leela was anguished to see the changed world around her, "the city metamorphosing into something very different from the Bombay of mills, factories and the workers, the Bombay of middle-class dreams and hard work that she had known and loved" (198). Though she was disillusioned with the trade unionism 'degenerating into violence and intimidation', in the words of the heroism of her life lived both for herself and for others. Her story in the words of Collette, "is a story of human potentiality and possibility" (2004: 77).

Madhu, who has always believed that women can never be free, changes her opinion: "knowing Leela and now Bai, I cannot go along with this idea. Both these women got for themselves the measure of freedom they needed, they worked for it. And they both knew the price they had to pay for it" (224). Leela put up with Paula and never showed her anger at her atrocious behaviour towards her. When she married Joe, she knew she had taken on the problem of Paula. Bai also paid her price. She was rejected by her daughter. Both these women accepted the consequences of their actions wholly and made no complaints. At the same time, both were victims of gender discrimination but it was their determination that led them to the realisation of their dreams. Even after years of working for the party, Leela was sidelined and could not reach the top of the hierarchy while a man, who worked under her, got there but she never complained. Only once when a woman, who was the widow of a member who had been killed, was selected as a candidate for a by-election, she said, "It seems you have got to become a widow for them to remember that you exist", (224) pointing at the chauvinism that ruled the party. She resigned from the party not because she was superseded but because she was disillusioned about being able to do anything from within the system.

Though Bai might not know the phrase 'gender discrimination', she was aware that it took a longer time for a woman to reach the top. Once Speaking of a young and swiftly rising instrumentalist, she gave a hint of it: "nowadays they become Ustads and Pandits even before they have proper moustaches" (224). But it was not a complaint. Both Leela and Savitribai never made complaints about the problems they had to face in their professional lives. To them, "these were part of the road they had chosen, they just had to be endured" (ibid.).

Githa Hariharan's *When Dreams Travel* takes up the age-old story of Scheherazade or Shahrzad; the female storyteller who tells Shahryar; an Arabian king a different story every night for a thousand and one nights as a means of delaying her death. As *The Arabian Nights* has developed out of an oral tradition, there have been many creators, retellers and rewriters of these stories. But most of them have reconstructed them as exciting and entertaining tales and Shahrzad as 'the exotic Scheherazade'. Githa Hariharan retells it as a story in which Shahrzad is not "a beautiful woman who told innocuous bed time stories in fabulous cloths" but a woman who is "like her own story, a survivor" (25). She is seen not as a myth but as a woman who asserted her power "over the blood thirsty sword" and brought "the Sultan to his senses" with "her ready tongue and cleverness" (21). With her sister Dunyazad, who was 'the audience, the prompter, the chorus, the heckler', Shahrzad told stories "that went so very near the sultan's sword; that touched its pointed tip and survived to vanquish him" (37).

Shahrzad is seen by Hariharan as 'a living legend' whose wit will "live on longer than any of her children or her grand children", her name like "a vine that creeps forward inch by inch growing from one millennium to another" and no story will be "made, told which cannot fit into the canvas she has stretched for a thousand and one nights" (273–274).

Hariharan's story begins where *The Arabian Nights* ends: "The story ends on stage. Off-stage it has just begun" (16). The novel is divided into two parts, the first is the retelling of *The Arabian Nights* through an unnamed third person narrator and the second is a series of stories that Shahrzad might have told. The stories are recalled by Dunyazad; Shahrzad's sister and Dilshad; a slavegirl with a view to replicate the voices of the past. Hariharan gives voice to Dunyazad, who is the silent accomplice in *The Arabian Nights,* to understand and articulate Shahrzad's voice. In the novel after the thousand and one nights are over, Shahrzad is shown to be missing and the king Shahryar, to satisfy his ego, is building a monument for her, assuming her to be dead. Interestingly, he is imprisoned in the tomb meant for Shahrzad by his son Umar. Though Dunyazad sees it as a kind of poetic justice, she feels that "reduced to invisibility, she (Shahrzad) is waiting for Dunyazad, her follower and accomplice to catch up with her and restore her to life" (113).

Dunyazad, who is more of a 'story seeker' than a storyteller, examines the story of Shahrzad 'from every point of view that occurs to her', searches it 'to light up all its remote corners' (115–116). Shahrzad is resurrected as a woman, giving this message to her descendants:

> I fought for myself, and yes, for you as well. And what will you do when your turn comes? When the drums roll and the sword blunted with age, the rusty axe, wake up to be freshly sharpened. (276)

When the novel opens, King Shahryar, who has murdered virgin brides consistently for three years before the appearance of Shahrzad, is shown to be at the centre of power. "Tall, firm-backed standing apart from everything" around him, he rules, "not over mere cities and fields but over his property. Not over men and women, but over his subjects" (8). He not only owns the land but also the people. The king, thus, represents authority. Women before Shahrzad had remained silent victims but Shahrzad not only saved her own life and the life of other women, she also created herself and recreated the world through the power of her words and emerged as a survivor.

It was under the shadow of death that Shahrzad told her stories. The sword which was "sheathed in the heart of the palace and unsheathed every dawn", could 'get her any day', but she was not to be defeated by "swords and whimsical notions of holder and held" (131). In the novel, Dunyazad, who relives her memory of Shahrzad, recalls 'the pregnant Shahrzad', her pain and suffering and also her immense courage which made it possible for her to get through. Shahrzad made a plan with Dunyazad so that the baby could be delivered with safety. She thought of telling a story with "an endless chain of marvels so that it will take her through to dawn" (121) and asked Dunyazad to "make appreciative noises and exclamations if she is breathless" (126). The pain tears her apart but she delivers the child while telling the king the story. The narrator in the novel first comments: "Though she has not yet triumphed, she has kept the murderous sword of the sultan at bay for nine long months, and she will die the death of a fighter who has fought to her last breath" but then makes an amendment: "... stop, she does not want to die. She wants the life of the child, but her own first" (128).

Of course, the basic urge was to live, but at the same time Shahrzad was a woman who did not want to live an anonymous and unfulfilled life. After the child was born, Dunyazad, who could not see her sister go on like this, brought with her one night a dagger hidden between the waistfolds of her skirt. She suggested Shahrzad to get rid of the sultan while he was getting ready to listen to her stories. Shahrzad refused by saying: "Here I am, talking for my life and yours, and you talk of more bloodshed? Look at this empty harem. Can't you hear its walls weep?" (131). Dunyazad knows that even if Shahrzad murders the king, she would still be a saviour, ridding Shahabad of a brutal king, but she also knows that women like Shahrzad "come alive only when there is danger at their heels and their blood races with terror" (132). They face the challenges of life and do not succumb to easy options. In Shahrazad's case it was creativity, born out of the struggle for life, which kept her alive.

So storytelling, no doubt, saved Shahrzad's life, it was also a strategy to "reclaim her history, write her body into cultural visibility and write the story of her body" (Farahani, on line version). Shahrzad gains her subjectivity not only through the power of her words but also through the power of her body. In this connection Moira Gatens writes:

> The human body is always a signified body and as such cannot be understood as a 'neutral object' ... Gender itself may be understood ... not as the effect of ideology or cultural values but as the way in which power takes hold of and constructs bodies in particular ways. Significantly, the sexed body can no longer be conceived as the unproblematic biological and factual base upon which gender is inscribed, but must itself be recognised as constructed by discourses and practices that take the body both as their target and as their vehicle of expression. (cited in Jain, 2002: 184)

It is not only the power of words, but also "the power of female sexuality of the body" that takes Shahrzad to the position of power (Githa Hariharan, *of Narratives, Narrators,* 2004: 384). Sexual activity parallels the narrative activity. Shahrzad never "paid as much attention to body as she has in the past few months" because she knew that like her storytelling performance, her body too "has to be coaxed and manipulated into a successful performance" (123). The two had gone together and storytelling had not in any way diminished 'the rights of bodily matters'. In this context, the definition of the word 'seduction' given by Fatima Mernissi is very relevant. In *Beyond the Veil: Male-Female Dynamic in Modern Muslim Society,* she writes:

> Seduction is a conflict strategy, a way of seeming to give of yourself, a procuring of great pleasure without actually giving. It is the art of abstaining from everything while playing on the promise of giving. (cited in Farahani, online version)

This is what Shahrzad did. She allowed herself to be subjugated only to create her subjectivity. Through storytelling, she encouraged not only the king's desire for another tale but also for her as a sexual being and thus created her subjectivity.

The novel is replete with metaphors that are associated with desire, physical desire as well as the desire for hearing more stories. Dunyazad's first sight of Shahryar is that "of a man in the thrall of desire. Or desire fulfilled" and sees him like "a stag that has escaped the tiger only to die of its wounds" (56). Without his royal robes and jewels, he is likened to 'a ragged hungry crow' whose 'thin vulnerable neck sheltered unprotected' on Shahrzad's shoulder who then 'stroked' his head, and 'soothed' him by saying: "One more story then, one more, and it will be dawn before you know it" (273).

Thus, in a society where women were oppressed and victimised, Shahrzad not only saved her life but also left a legacy;

a legacy in which women could see themselves as human beings, rather than as victims. Fataneh Farahani in her article "Shahrzad's Guile" pays tributes to her:

> Shahrzad is a voice from insight the harem that reaches outside. In Shahrzad's time no woman had a voice or images. Before Shahrzad there was a masculine history that did not allow women to be visible. Women's experiences in Iran continue to be rendered invisible, although the example of Shahrzad reveals the opportunity for resistance to such silencing. Shahrzad made women's lives visible in *Thousand and One Nights*. She was a protester who felt the shadow of the death all the time. The shadow of death and the king's power made her to feel hesitant all the time, but she did not allow the king to see that. Instead she made him hesitate each night when he contemplated whether or not he would have her killed. It was in those moments of hesitation that Shahrzad took the opportunity to give herself voice and make the king confront his own uncertainty. Her courage has meant that there are heirs to her legacy, voices to speak who also refuse to be silent. As one of Shahrzad's heirs, now living in the one thousand and second night, I reclaimed her voice as a tribute for the voice she gave to me.(online version)

The story of Shakutai, embedded in *The Binding Vine* (Deshpande), is also a story of struggle for survival and this struggle is not just for economic survival but also for "the preservation of human dignity and in the end some human warmth and ability to reach out to others" (Dhar, 1996: 105). Shakutai is a working class woman. Soon after marriage, her husband leaves for Bombay, assuring her that he would soon take her away. She waits almost a year and then follows him to Bombay on her own where she discovers that he is an alcoholic and does not want to work. He remains idle while she takes up all kinds of jobs available to her. In fact she never minded working: "I am never frightened of work, I am used to it. I did all the work without complaining. But ..." (110). What she minded the most was her husband's making her sleep with him in an open passage outside the room of his cousin where people kept coming and going, indifferent to both her feelings and the presence of others. Not only that, he leaves her after she has given birth to three children and starts living with another woman. She reconciles to this and goes on with life bravely. She refuses to take any financial assistance from her father. She does all kinds of work, and even looks after a paralytic old woman, "cleaning up her filth ..." so that her children could grow up, could go to school, and live better than her (111). She has a sense of self-respect also. She buys them a TV so that they do not have to go to other people's houses to watch it.

Life continues to be a great struggle for Shakutai. She is very much relieved when Sulu and her husband take on the responsibility of Kalpana; her daughter for she thinks that she will have all that she herself never has had, "education, a good life, a good marriage, respect from others ..." (111). But all her dreams are shattered when Kalpana is raped by Sulu's husband. Sulu commits suicide while Kalpana goes into coma. This is the most traumatic experience that one can have and though after this Shakutai finds it difficult to go on, she soon overcomes it: "You can never opt out, you can never lay it down, the burden of belonging to human race" (202). Urmila finds her getting on with her chores in the morning and sees in her a kind of resoluteness. Earlier Shakutai had tried to hide that her daughter was raped. She was afraid that it would bring disgrace to her and would also make it difficult for her younger daughter to get married. She had also tried to hide that it was her sister's husband who raped her. But realisation dawns upon her that "her daughter's tragedy and her sister's death can no longer be shrouded in silence" (203). Here it would be pertinent to mention, by a way of contrast, that Gopal renounces family life in *A Matter of Time* well before the period prescribed by the *Brahad Aranyaka Upanishad.* Deshpande refers to in the novel, a behaviour rather inexplicable in the context of a culture where responsibilities outweigh desires. In fact, Gopal is Deshpande's only male character who gets the maximum sympathy and discursive space in all of her fictional writings, and the other characters' attitude, except for Aru's occasionally harsh criticism, is also made relatively uncritical. Gopal's reflections imbued with the philosophies, stories and legends from Indian mythology and religion in an attempt to seek answer to the meaning of life and the turmoil within him seem to draw a kind of ambivalent sympathy from the authorial sensibility.

Shakutai is different from Deshpande's other working-class women who, despite being consistently oppressed by their husbands, value their 'mangalsutra', as for example, Jeeja in *That Long Silence.* One of Shakutai's dreams was to have her 'mangalsutra' made in gold but she gives up this idea: "the man himself is so worthless, why should I bother to have this thing made in precious gold?" (110)

Shakutai has an immense capacity to go beyond her personal grief and reach out to others. Even after her daughter is raped and is lying in the hospital in coma, she goes to the help of a young girl, consoles her with 'encouraging murmurs', because "the girl is frightened, she has never seen illness" (109). The story of Shakutai reminds us what Shashi Deshpande has written in *A Matter of Time:*

> If it is indeed true that we are bound to our destinies, then there is no point struggling against them, even then this remains-that we do not submit passively or cravenly but with dignity and strength. (246)

In the story "The Day of the Golden Deer" also included in *The Stone Women*, Shashi Deshpande's Sita, when she is rejected by Ram, discards a sense of helplessness:

> Fate! I knew the word would come. But I will have nothing to do with it. I cannot believe in it. We cannot escape the consequences of our actions, of our wrong, that way. That is the easy way out. It is not the fate that shapes our lives, but our wills, our actions. (70–71)

Shashi Deshpande's characters struggle to become their own refuge. Towards the end of the novel Shakutai gives this life sustaining message: "The main urge is always to survive" (203).

Shakutai stands in direct contrast to her sister, Sulu who used to be a lively woman but who changes after her marriage as she fails to have a child. She lives in constant fear: "what if he does not like this, what if he wants that, what if he is angry with me, what if he throws me out" (115). Shakutai does not like her living this sort of life. She says to Urmila, the protagonist in the novel: "Nobody should live like that, so full of fears. What kind of life is it?" (115). In the end Sulu commits suicide. The shock of her husband's ghastly act, the sense of betrayal she experiences and the guilt she lives with make it impossible for her to continue with the act of living.

Shakutai's story of survival and courage is the story of a fictional character but another similar real-life story is that of Baby Halder, a working class woman whose life has been equally oppressive but who, like Shakutai, does not give up and faces the challenges of life bravely. Oppressed by her husband, Baby Halder's mother leaves the house and the father remarries. Baby Halder has to give up her studies. She is married at the age of twelve and becomes a mother at the age of fourteen. Being persistently tormented by her husband, she comes to Delhi on her own with her three children where she finds a job of a maid. As she does not get time to look after her children, who are locked up on the roof of the house, she gives up the job and takes up another job in the house of Prabodh Kumar, a professor of anthropology and the grandson of Premchand. While dusting the books in his library, she is drawn towards the books in Bengali. Seeing her interest, Prof. Kumar not only encourages her to read but also encourages her to write with the result that she writes her autobiography in Bengali which has been translated into English as *A Life Less Ordinary* by Urvashi Butalia. In the autobiography, Baby Halder narrates the hardships she has faced but she does not indulge in self-pity nor does she make any complaint about her fate. The story of Baby Halder, though it raises several questions about the fate of the millions of working class women in India and the treatment that is meted out to them, is essentially "a story of courage under fire" (from the book review by R. Krithika, *The Hindu*, April 4, 2006).

The embedded stories of survival function in multiple ways. They take the novel away from being an individualised narrative. The stories of Savitribai and Leela are the stories of all those who reach 'beyond their grasp'. Usha Bande is absolutely right when she says that Shashi here "seems to direct her attention to the higher issues of human struggle through individual strivings" (2005: 193). Bande compares Deshpande to George Eliot who, in her letter to Charles Bay, writes: "The only effect I ardently long to produce by my writings, is that those who read them should be better able to imagine and to feel the pains and the joys of those who differ from themselves in everything but the broad facts of being struggling human creatures" (cited in Bande, 2005: 203). Shashi Deshpande too, in her conversation with Vanamala Viswanatha, says: "I want to reach a stage where I can write about human beings and not about women to men ..."

(Pathak, 1998: 237). In *Small Remedies* she reaches that stage where she is more concerned with issues regarding the human self and not just the female self, more concerned "with the human condition than just the female psyche and condition" (Shashi Deshpande, *The Hindu* September 5, 2004).

The embedded stories also introduce parallels and contrasts making the narrative structure more complex. For instance, in *Small Remedies,* while the stories of Savitribai and Leela run parallel, they have been placed against the story of Madhu which is the main narrative in the novel. The lives of Savitribai and Leela, lived to the utmost, stand in direct contrast to the life of Madhu who has lived for and through her child. After Madhu has probed into their lives, she comes to see her obsession with motherhood as 'a small centre, a vast exclusion'. They also help Madhu to come out of her grief over her son's death. She realises that though death changes all, the flow of life goes on:

> I thought that when you lost everything, there would be no more fear. But when all is gone, there is still life itself, life pursuing its own ends of survival, of growth. Ultimately it is the body that dictates to us, coercing us into its purposes of living and growing. Survival is all, survival is what matters above everything. (201)

Similarly, Urmila (*The Binding Vine*), after she has seen Shakutai's strength to withstand hardships, comes to terms with the death of her daughter. She also learns from Shakutai to go beyond one's own pain and suffering and to reach out to others. She can see that there is the 'spring of life', the love and sharing of joys and sorrows that bind us together and help us to come out of our personal sorrows.

References

Bande, Usha. "Resistance and Reconciliation: Shashi Deshpande's *A Matter of Time and Small Remedies*", *Writing Difference: The Novels of Shashi Deshpande*. Ed. Chanchala K. Naik. New Delhi: Pencraft International, 2005.

Collette, Anne. "The Relationship between Existentialism, Materialism and Feminism in the Novels of Shashi Deshpande", *Desert in Bloom*. Ed. Meenakshi Bharat. New Delhi: Pencraft International. 2004.

De Beauvoir, Simone. *The Second Sex*. Harmondsworth: Penguin, 1972.

Deshpande, Shashi. "Telling Our Own Stories", *Writing from the Margin*. New Delhi: Penguin, 2003.

——. "A Conversation with June Gaur". *The Hindu*, Sept.5, 2004.

——. "Denying the Otherness". Interview by Geetha Gangadharan, *The Fiction of Shashi Deshpande*. Ed. R.S. Pathak. New Delhi: Creative Books, 1998.

——. "A Woman's World ... All The Way!" Interview with Vanamala Viswanatha, *The Fiction of Shashi Deshpande*. Ed. R.S. Pathak. New Delhi: Creative Books, 1998.

Dhar, T.N. "Wrestle with Mesmosyne: Self and Human Dignity", *A Bird in the House: Theory and Interpretation of Literature*. Ed. Charu Sheel. New Delhi: Anmol Publication, 1996.

Farahani, Fataneh. "Shahrzad's Guile". June 2,2006 http://tns. Se/Kf/eng/fataneh. Htm.

Hariharan, Githa "How I Write and Why? Githa Hariharan Answers", *Of Narratives, Narrators*. Ed. Rajul Bhargava and Shubhshree. New Delhi and Jaipur: Rawat Publications, 2004.

Jain, Jasbir. "The Body in/of the Text: Structure and Meaning in Women's Narratives", *Gender and Narrative*. Eds. Jasbir Jain and Supriya Agarwal. New Delhi and Jaipur: Rawat Publications, 2002.

——. *Gendered Realities, Human Spaces: Writings of Shashi Deshpande*. New Delhi and Jaipur: Rawat Publications, 2003.

——. "Cultural Rooting/Routing through English", *Writing Difference: The Novels of Shashi Deshpande*. Ed. Chanchala K. Naik. New Delhi: Pencraft International, 2005.

Hall, Stuart. "Ethnicity: Identity and Difference", *Beyond Borders: A Cultural Reader*. Eds. Randall Bass and Joy Young. New York: Houghton Mifflin Co., 2003.

Krithika, R. "A Story of Courage under Fire", Review of *A Life Less Ordinary* (originally in Bengali, Translated. in English by Urvashi Butalia). *The Hindu*, 4/7/2006.

Naik, K. Chanchala. "*Moving On*: In Search of Individual Autonomy and Self-Realization", *Writing Difference: The Novels of Shashi Deshpande*. Ed. Chanchala K. Naik. New Delhi: Pencraft International, 2005.

Sartre, Jean-Paul. "Existentialism is Humanism", *Existentialism from Dostoevsky to Sartre*. Ed. Walter Kaufmall. New York: New American Library, 1975.

CHAPTER 5

Storytelling and Storytellers

Shashi Deshpande and Githa Hariharan have been greatly influenced by India's timeless storytelling traditions. Besides being exposed to the tradition of English writers such as Jane Austen, Charles Dickens and Shakespeare, they have also been familiar with the traditions of Indian writers writing in English as well as in the regional languages. One more tradition that has been available to them and has fascinated them is India's oral tradition. The impact of this tradition can be seen in the way storytelling constitutes a very significant part of their works. In "Discreet Thoughts" Githa Hariharan writes:

> Personally, I feel I have three rich legacies to draw on as a writer. First there is the long Indian tradition of storytelling and the various streams of the literatures in Indian languages.

> Second, there is the body of English and European writers who made up our 'canon' in school and college. And Third, we have the alternative prophets, writers like G.V. Desai and later Salman Rushdie who made the parallel legacies in vibrant work in tune with our times. (2004: 215)

Due to illiteracy, India's narrative tradition has been largely oral. Stories were handed down from one generation to another mostly by word of mouth and this form of oral tradition was very much in practice. Apart from the epics the *Mahabharata*, and the *Ramayana* which were recited, the stories in the form of fables were told in villages with a moral at the end of each tale. Teachings of Buddha were also disseminated in the form of stories. Gradually the written form absorbed the oral tradition.

Though storytelling has its roots in a pre-literate, primarily oral tradition but the urge to tell stories is something irrepressible, something that we cannot dispense with. Emphasizing this point J.H. Miller writes:

> Nothing seems more natural and universal to human being than telling story. Surely there is no human culture, however "primitive", without its stories and habits of storytelling, its myths of the origin of the world, its legends of the tribe or group of stories about folk heroes ... . From our earliest childhood we hear stories and learn to repeat them. As adults, we hear, read, see, and tell stories all day long-for example, in the newspaper, on the television, in encounters with coworkers or family members. In a continuous silent internal activity, we tell stories to ourselves all day long ... . At night we sleep and our unconscious minds tell us stories in our dreams. (1995: 66)

More than any other form of communication, the telling of stories is an integral and essential part of the human life. It imposes certain order on the varied experiences and gives meaning and coherence to them. Shlomith Rimmon-Kenan in *Narrative Fiction* writes that "Narration is in no way restricted to literature. In order to make sense of experiences, people consciously or unconsciously, audibly or inaudibly, tell stories to themselves as well as to others" (2001: 147). Rukmini Bhaya Nair in her book *Narrative Gravity: Conversation, Cognition, Culture* also affirms that people do not see and understand the world around them until it is put in narrative form. She sees narrative as a species of natural theory designed "to probe experiences and create competing theories about the world, especially, the world of emotional experience which is so crucial to cultural survival, and present explanations of the enigmas we encounter in the daily business of living" (2003: 2).

Storytelling, thus, is a primordial, crucial human activity. It is an intrinsic and basic form of communication through which we assess and interpret events and experiences from lusterless moments of daily life to the moments grand in nature. Malleability is the characteristic of this oral tradition and this is because, whether spoken or written, it implies someone who speaks or writes it. Robert Scholes and Robert Kellogg, while distinguishing narrative from other genres, write:

> By narrative we mean all those literary works which are distinguished by two characteristics: the presence of a story and a storyteller. A drama is a story without a storyteller; in it characters act out directly … . A lyric, like a drama, is a direct presentation, in which a single actor, the poet or his surrogate, sings, or muses, or speaks for us to hear or overhear. Add a second speaker and we move toward drama … . Let the speaker begin to tell of an event, and we move toward narrative. For writing to be narrative no more and no less than a teller and a tale are required. (1966: 4)

A story comes into being only when it is mediated by a voice. It is this mediation which makes a story infinitely malleable. H. Porter Abbott in his book *The Cambridge Introduction to Narrative* makes an important distinction between story, narrative discourse and narrative. According to him, while a story is an event or a sequence of events (the action), narrative discourse is those events as represented and narrative is the representation of those events, consisting of story and narrative discourse. It is the narrative discourse which makes a story malleable. No two tellings of a story will ever be the same. In this connection Karl Kroeber in *Retelling/Rereading: The Fate of Storytelling in Modern Times* also writes:

> Every storytelling performance is unique, and the narrative's pre-eminent accomplishment is the articulation of meaning for contingent events without gainsaying their contingency. Stories are always retold and are *meant* to be retold, reheard, reread, that narrative is a repeating form of discourse—in which every repetition is unique. (1992: 1)

Even while dealing with the same story, there can be many different versions, many discrepancies and inconsistencies, yet the core of the story can be retained. This paradox makes storytelling an important mode of cultural discourse as it can preserve ideas, beliefs and convictions without their being hardened into dogma. Since narrative is the discourse most amenable to translative adaptations, stories have helped us cross socio-cultural boundaries. It is through narratives that the great cultures and religions of the world have articulated, consolidated and disseminated their influence. Rukmini Bhaya Nair in "Narrative Evolution: In Human Cognition and Across All Cultures" also writes that a "good story in any culture is one which converts a talk into text so that it is adapted to being carried and reused" (2004: 62). Karl Kroeber compares stories to plant species "that move readily but unobtrusively over surprising obstacles, including vast spans of time and space, quietly adapting to foreign environments, and then changing those environments" and thus they permit simultaneous retention and revision of its peculiarities" (1992: 3). The Cinderella story, for example, or the Faust story is traceable in almost all the cultures throughout the world in different versions and yet can be recognised as the same story. Each story establishes its own history which is preserved by being made anew with every telling.

'Openness' is particularly characteristic of storytelling as it is intrinsically a co-creative process in which both the teller and the listener play their roles. While a story is being told, the listener is not passive. Though, apparently, he surrenders himself to the flow of the narrator's words, he is simultaneously processing what he 'receives', based on the performance by the teller and on his past experiences, beliefs and understanding. As a result, the completed story happens in the mind of the listener, unique and personal for each individual.

Just as no one story is the 'definite' story, similarly every story implies other stories. Kroeber writes:

> Storytelling is a proliferative activity. Inconclusive, question-provoking endings merely render visible this fecundity, that the closer inherent to narrative as a whole creates new openings, possibilities for other stories that, in fact, are a major empowerment of any story's successful social functioning. The central purpose of storytelling is to facilitate tellings. The end of any story makes possible more storytelling which is encouraged by whatever is enigmatic or debatable in a particular conclusion. (1992: 72)

Even if the ending of a given story is conclusive, it does not and cannot exclude the possibility of a subsequent story. There are always gaps in a story and the gaps always remain open, no matter how detailed the presentation is. The gaps give opportunity to the listener or the reader to recreate the story. In the opinion of J.H. Miller, even perfectly conceived stories fail to "accomplish successfully their allotted function" and they leave "some uncertainty or contains some loose end" (1995: 72). The same idea is expressed by Wolfgang when he writes:

> No tale can be told in its entirety. Indeed it is only through inevitable omissions that a story will gain dynamism. Thus whenever the flow is interrupted and we are led off in unexpected directions, the opportunity is given to us to bring into play our own faculty for establishing connections—for filling in gaps left by the text itself. (1971: 285)

Storytelling, thus, demands interpretation, but at the same time it resists a final, absolute interpretation and renews itself by means of its gaps and absences. Similarly, as we grow more familiar with a story, the questions and problems posed by it may not necessarily disappear. On the contrary, they may deepen and may require a return to the story, another retelling or rereading of it, revealing depths and dimensions that we might have hitherto failed to see.

Narratives, therefore, as Rajul Bhargava has stated, "though basic and obvious, they are neither 'simple' texts nor 'simply' told—there are ways and ways of telling and ways and ways in which the most simple of stories are embedded in a network of relations that are astounding in their complexity" (2004: Front Flap). It is against this backdrop that I propose to explore storytelling in Shashi Deshpande and Githa Hariharan.

Both Shashi Deshpande and Githa Hariharan believe that stories are never finished. In an interview with Anuradha Marwah, Githa Hariharan says: "It is in the nature of these stories all of us hear and retell that they are never finished. There is no authoritative version. They must be twisted and retold for our times and lives" (*Pioneer*, February 7, 1999). In *Moving On* Deshpande also writes: "... the story goes on. An endless chain, it is not over, the story goes on" (41). Both the writers explore the nature of memory and its role in storytelling. Memory does not always tell the same story. When we recall an incident and try to recreate it, 'never the same returns' as the selective process has already come into existence which replaces simple, automatic, instinctual reactions. While using adjectives like 'incomplete', 'personal', 'fragmentary' and 'unreliable' to define the nature of memory, Jasbir Jain points out that "our conscious responses at a particular time may later be pushed underground, hidden, repressed or camouflaged and then pushed into the unconscious" (1987: 131). Maud Ellmann, who is of the same opinion, also writes, "If memory is constructed in the present, the past, as such, can never be recovered. Remembering becomes dismembering" (cited in Bijay Danta, 2005: 214).

Usually we remember what we want to and most of the time we remember only those experiences which are either happy or painful and that too come in fragments, from a subtly different vintage point each time. A very apt illustration of this is *The Binding Vine* where Kishore, Vanna, and Urmi recollect an incident that happened in their childhood and all three recollect it differently, making Urmi wonder: "Three people, three different versions of an event, almost three different events. Where is the truth? Perhaps the fact is that we all of us create our own truths, shaping them to our needs, in particular the need to be able to live comfortably with ourselves, with those we love and need" (54–55). In *That Long Silence* also, if on the one hand, Mohan, while relating the story of his childhood to Jaya, recollects how his father had kicked him when he had fallen ill, Jaya's memories of her father-in-law, on the other hand, are different. She remembers him as a gentle, old and frail person and finds it "hard to reconcile that crude gesture with the man she saw and knew" (35). She creates her own story based on her memory and understanding of the situation. Recollections and retellings, thus, produce not only multiple but even contradictory versions. Each memory of each person carries its own truth which varies not only with different people but is often at variance with itself. Madhu's memories of Savitribai (*Small Remedies*), as she recalls one incident after the other, undercut each other and the story goes on multiplying endlessly. According to Jerome Singer, memory constantly replaces one picture with another as it is not simply, to quote him, "an inert storage box like computer's, but a system in constant motion" (1975: 251). While one is considering what came before or after, it snatches away the picture to replace it with another and has 'the powers of duplication'. At the same time, like 'a big fat parasite', memory never leaves one. In the words of Madhu in *Small Remedies*:

> How could I ever long for amnesia? Memory, capricious and unreliable though it is, ultimately carries its own truth within it. As long as there is memory, there is always the possibility of retrieval, as long as there is memory, loss is never total. (324)

Therefore, the story that memory tells is neither complete nor is ever finished. In *The Ghosts of Vasu Master* Vasu as a story-teller comments upon this aspect of memory and its role in storytelling:

> I hear a voice from among you ask: Is this the end of the story? It is, it could be if I could also say the story is complete. But just when I am done with remembering, when I round it all off, put an end to it, I see that flash again, the burst of life when everything blurs for a second. And then it all begins again, the tragi-comic antics of an apparently random sample of humanity, a streetful of passing faces, it continues, picks up a thread and ties others into intimate knots, the pictures moving one at the tail of what went before, like the partly hidden view of a wheel. Like a serpent, gliding past silently, sinuously, taking care never to leave me too far behind. (274)

Memory continuously weaves sinuous strands till they are inseparable and transfigures each line of experience. Not only this, memory constantly interrupts the linearity, "pushes and pulls back and forth with complete disregard for sequence, sometimes even meaning", and "jumps from one event to another". One has to constantly be "on the alert, edit, correct memory if one is to make a coherent narrative and all one can attempt is the semblance of a whole" (*The Ghosts of Vasu Master*: 235).

The same view is expressed by Laurence Lerner. According to him, each narrative is "a blend of observation, memory and imagination" ((1988: 12). Saleem Sinai in *The Midnight's Children* also says that what he is narrating is "Memory's truth because memory has its own special kind. It selects, eliminates, alters, exaggerates, minimises, glorifies, and vilifies also but in the end creates its own reality, its heterogeneous but usually coherent version of events" (1981: 211). So what is narrated is the 'truth' of one's memory, memory which is given shape by one's imagination as it is 'fractured' and 'fragmented', 'compounded' by one's perception and observation of events. In *Small Remedies* Madhu reinforces this idea:

> You can't change events, events are immovable, rooted, like those road rollers that stayed for months at one spot in Neemgaon. But you can change the way you look at events. (165–66)

In short, there can never be an authoritarian version of a story or an event. Each time "the lens are changed, a different perspective emerges" (Jain, 1987: 130). The same story, when narrated by different genders, may differ in perspectives and perceptions. Mohan in *That Long Silence*, while narrating the story of his mother sitting in front of the fire waiting for her husband who always came late and still wanted his food hot, sees in the story the strength of his mother. Jaya, on the other hand, sees in the story a struggle "so bitter that silence was the only weapon. Silence and surrender" (36). Perspectives and perceptions may differ not only with different people and different genders but also with the same person as he perceives an event/situation differently at different phases of his or her life. The protagonist Manjari in *Moving On* (Shashi Deshpande), as she recollects the memories of her childhood, realises that things are coming to her 'differently' as she recollect the memories of her childhood. As an adult, she sees her parents through a different lens and the truth dawns upon her that the parents of her childhood were "figures I had created for my own purposes, they were my childhood pacifiers I hugged for security" (21).

In Shashi Deshpande, the stories that are being told are simultaneously being revised or even reversed as the characters go back to their personal past as well as to that of others. Their understanding of the same person or of the same event continues to change or even reverse. In *Moving On* Manjari, who had thought her father "a quiet, sedate man", comes to sees him as "a man who was something of a rebel" (4). In *Small Remedies,* Madhu first sees Savitribai as a self-centred woman who even disowned her daughter to fulfil her dreams but then her perception changes and she sees her as a woman who reached 'beyond her grasp'. In her conversation with Lakshmi Holmstrom Shashi Deshpande says: "Is there any single point in our lives at which one can truly say, 'That is all over?' One moves on from any decision" (1998: 247). Here what is being emphasized by her is the fluidity of reality which is what she emphasises in her stories as well.

Small Remedies is a kind of metafictional text, a work that reflects on "the impossibility of ever capturing in words the truths about any life" (Mukherjee, 2004: 174). At the very outset

Deshpande sets the metafictional tone of the novel: "This is Som's story, or rather Joe's story as related to us by Som. To me the two man, narrator and object are equally part of the story" (1). This is a thoughtful meditation on creating art and writing fiction. The narrator cannot separate the tale from the way he tells it. The power of the storyteller is to create art out of life, a process which is the subject of *Small Remedies*. In the novel Madhu; the writer-narrator is assigned the task of writing the biography of Savitribai. Savitribai was her neighbour in her childhood and Savitribai's daughter Munni was her friend. But in her conversation with Madhu, Savitribai does not mention her daughter nor does she show that she has recognised Madhu. She does not mention even Ghulam Saab, the man who helped Savitribai in her pursuit of music and with whom she shared her life after she had left her husband. But it becomes increasingly clear to Madhu that she "cannot be the invisible narrator ... the child who knew Bai, the girl who knew Munni, the woman who is constantly aware of Bai's blanketing of Munni's name-they are the part of the book, they will be part of Bai's story and it cannot be avoided" (162). Each session with Savtribai triggers off Madhu's own memories connected with Munni and Ghulam Saab. Though Madhu feels that Savitribai has a right to her privacy, to protect her life from 'public gaze', but then she feels she cannot write "with this huge hole in the centre of her life" (177). She constantly oscillates between her memories of Savitribai and what Savitribai herself tells her about her own life.

While relating her story, Savitribai follows one straight line of her pursuit of music and her Guruji, making "a deliberate progress through events" (165). But Madhu knows that she cannot write a chronological account of her life for:

> We see our lives through memory and memories are fractured, fragmented, almost always cutting across. Even to write our own stories, we need to invent. Like fiction writers, like

> historians, the teller of a story needs to construct a plausible narrative. How else do you connect but by imagining? (165)

It is here that Shashi Deshpande moves from the nature of memory and its multiplicity to the inevitability of fiction in any narrative. What Savitribai remembers is all premeditated and the story that she tells is 'the rehearsed story' (28). She remembers only what she wants to and deliberately obliterates her daughter and Ghulam Saab. But Madhu is aware of the gaps in her story and if Bai does not open her mouth, she has to 'fill in the blanks herself' (129).

Madhu first 'records' Savitribai's life story and allows her to speak from her own perspective. As she replays the tape, she notices the silences and the pauses. This gives Madhu "a sudden glimpse of a human being behind that shield like seeing the eyes of a burqua cloaked woman through the eye-slits" (176–177). Madhu is reminded of Savitribai's face while she was relating how she was interrupted by her grandmother in the midst of a song and was asked to stop singing. Though she remains silent about the hardships that she has suffered in her pursuit of music, the pause in the tape at this point allows for the hidden truth to emerge.

Whatever Savitribai tells her is one of the many aspects of her life and therefore has to be taken note of but then this is not the only truth about her life. In *Moving On* also, as Manjari goes through her father's diary, she realises that 'baba is only giving her *his* picture'. She then comments: "But can there be any one truth about people? People are complex, undecipherable, protean—there is no absolute about them" (21). The act of self-revelation is in itself a complex one. In the words of Jaya in *That Long Silence*:

> Self-revelation is a cruel process. The real picture, the real 'you' never emerges. Looking for it is as bewildering as trying

> to know how you really look. Ten difference mirrors show you ten different faces ... . The mirror is always treacherous. It shows you only what you want to see. And, perhaps, others too see in your face only what they want to see. (1–2)

Here, Shashi Deshpande points out that there are many selves of a person and so when a person tells about himself or herself or about others, the whole truth does not come out. For Madhu, who places motherhood above everything else, Savitribai is primarily Munni's mother and then a singer. As such, she cannot give 'a minor role' to Munni in the story. She first sees in Bai a cruel mother but her view and perception continue to change as she recalls one incident after another. Memory thus constantly interrupts the linear movement of time. Madhu comes across several selves of Savitribai and wonders:

> Which is the real Bai? The pampered child? The young girl who discovered what her life was going to be? The young woman who abandoned her child and eloped with her lover? The great musician, the successful Savitribai Indoreker. All of them, of course. It is always a palimpsest, so many layers, one superimposed on another, none erased, all of them still there. (283)

The problem that Madhu faces is which self to write about. As she puts it, there are three books:

> Firstly, there is Bai's book, the book Bai wants to be written, in which she is the heroine, the spot light shining on her and her alone, all the shadows kept out of sight, back stage.
> Then there's Maya's and Yogi's book. A controversial one, Trendy. Politically correct, with a feminist slant. A book that will sell.
> And there is my book, the one I am is still looking for. It is evading me, not giving me a hold anywhere. (125)

Hasina, who is Gulam Saab's granddaughter and who loves and respects him, gives Madhu her own story and she wants Madhu 'to write the *truth*'. Madhu is reminded of "the seven blind men trying to describe the elephant, each one making a different discovery about the animal, each convinced that his knowledge about the elephant is the entire truth" (278). She feels the enormous power of her words: "Yes, the words that present Bai to the world will be mine" (162). In this connection Patricia Waugh writes:

> The simple notion that language passively reflects a coherent, meaningful and 'objective' world is no longer tenable. Language is an independent, self-contained system which generates its own 'meanings'. (2002: 239)

It is with her words that Savitribai builds 'a huge cutout of an artist, a musician' and it is with her words that Madhu can 'sculpt' the great singer into the image she designs for her:

> I can take over Bai's life and make of it through my words what I want. I can trap her into an image I create, seal her into an identity I make for her. The power of the writer is the power of the creator. Yes, I can do much. I can make Bai the rebel who rejected the conventions of her times. The feminist who lived her life on her terms The great artist who struggled and sacrificed every thing in the cause of art and the woman who gave up every thing—a comfortable home, a husband and a family—for love. (166)

But then Madhu realises that it is not a matter of making choices. Her integrity lies in discovering a truth which will 'encompass all the different bits of knowledge' offered to her: "The tail, the trunk, the ears, the legs—yes, I have to put them together. I have to create an elephant out of these disparate bits" (278). Shashi Deshpande here, through her writer-protagonist-narrator, also gives a clue to her approach to writing. The writer has to transcend his/her personal feelings so that he/she can be truer to life. As a writer Madhu succeeds in doing so and by doing so she asserts the strength of which Shashi Deshpande mentioned in the opening paragraph of *That Long Silence* "To achieve something ... you have got to be hard and ruthless .... There is no other way of being a saint. Or a painter. A writer." By presenting different selves of Savitribai and the different versions of her story that emerge from different perspectives, Shashi Deshpande stresses the multiplicity of the self and the plurality of the truth.

Githa Hariharan's *When Dreams Travels* which reworks *The Thousand and One Nights,* though it embodies several other aspects, is essentially a book about 'hows' and 'whys' of storytelling. The novel explores memory; both as a reservoir and a manipulator of history and desire as a motivation for storytelling. It also develops the theme of the power of storytelling.

It is under the shadow of death that Shahrzad tells her stories. The more Shahrzad can recall, invent and imagine, the more she is insured against her death. Rukmini Bhaya Nair in her article "Narrative Evolution" observes that though "narrative is an evolutionary linguistic structure designed to facilitate cultural crossovers, but what makes it a 'discourse universal' is its play, its constant shadow jousts with death" (2004: 62). John Berger also referred to the figure of the storyteller as 'death's secretary'. Storytelling, thus, becomes "a mode of sustaining life, of keeping death at bay" (Nair, 2004: 64). In the novel, after thousand and one nights are over, Sultan asks Shahrzad "where did all those dreams come from" (20). She answers: "Only those locked up in hovels and dungeons and palaces can see and hear these dreams. Only those whose necks are naked and at risk can understand them" (ibid.). Here, Githa

Hariharan emphasises the immediacy and urgency also as the motivation for storytelling.

The stories that Shahrzad tells are half-remembered and half-imagined. She relates all that she has heard but she also unleashes the power of an invention-embellished memory. Not only this, she even 'plunders' from another narrative that comes to her mind. She sometimes 'slips someone else's passing idea into her narrative', or 'cribs a phrase or two, sometimes an entire frame from other narratives'. But she knows that "she is safe—no one looks at a nose or an eye out of the context of a face, or at a solitary balcony or pillar on an entire edifice. The synthesis will be hers and in that sense, the authorship which gives her a sense of power" (133).

Here, Githa Hariharan is stressing several things—the role of memory; the need for imagination and invention in a story or in any work of art, the importance of narrative skill even if the story is old or the ideas borrowed. She illustrates her point by comparing and contrasting the 'womanly fabricator' Shahrzad and the sultan "the builder who strips others' creations of what takes his fancy to build monuments for his own times" (133). Both Shahrzad and the sultan are 'fabricators' but with a difference. Sultan's reconstructions are mere 'phantoms', whereas Shahrzad's reconstructions make her 'a great builder' because they are not mere copies, but are mixed with invention and innovation. In her paper presented in a workshop on the art and craft of story writing, Mridula Garg says:

> A story is crafted/created when we go beyond the actual experience, mix it with other memories lying dormant, spice it up with a fair dose of imagination and serve it as an experienced reality more believable than the shallow reality around us. In the absence of craft we would, at best, relate our experiences as anecdotes and memoirs. (Creative Writing Workshop, December 9, 2005)

In the case of Shahrzad, her very survival depends upon her ability to catch and hold the interest of the king. She needs to create a sense of anticipation in the king, something that makes him eager to hear the rest of the stories. She also needs to create an illusion that she is telling a story which she happened to see or hear. In other words, the rendering of stories should be such that the king takes it, to borrow a phrase from Shlomith Rimmon, "an authoritarian account of the fictional truth" (2001: 101). In other words, the listener's confidence in the integrity of the storyteller is as crucial as the story's merit and the excitement it generates. Shahrzad succeeds not only in arousing king's interest but also in winning his trust in the authenticity of her tales and thus she insures the continuation of the narrative act and also of her life. Not only that, her method of narrating it is so unique and powerful that it changes the relationship between the two. It is Shahrzad who "holds the scene and is gifted with movement" whereas the king "Ruler of Shahbad, lord of this palace, its dome, shaded terraces, arch windowed upper rooms, its hidden dungeons" (43) is "bewitched into waiting, listening posture" (7). She takes the king to a world where "his rule and his rules are alien and where he is so entranced by her tales that she can rule him and can teach him how to be a subject before he again becomes the master of his fate" (Nafisi: on line version). He turns into a passive and addictive listener and learns for the first time to listen to a woman.

Michel Foucault stated, 'Knowledge is Power' and compared it with 'Might is Right'. He further observed that this 'Might' of 'Might is Right' was not at all different from the 'power' in 'Knowledge is Power' (cited in Lydia, 2000: 5). The only difference is that in one case it is the physical force, while in the other it is the mental force. In Shahrzad's case, it was the mental force which imposed itself on the physical force of the king. In the novel, when the thousand and one nights are over, the sultan and his brother are also shown to be asking Shahrzad,

"Where did all those stories come from. Shahzaman and I have read and studied more than you have. Certainly we have travelled more, seen marvels and lands and wickedness, you can only imagine" (19–20). She replies, "I don't have a sword, so it seems I cannot rule, I cannot travel, I don't care to weep. But I can dream" (20). So it is with her power of words and imagination that "the sultan Shahrayr, the all powerful antagonist is brought to his knees without resorting to his own brand of weapons" (132). The novel, thus, develops the theme of the power of storytelling and shows how storytelling plays a manipulative or liberating role in the power struggle.

In addition to all this, another important aspect of storytelling in both Shashi Deshpande and Githa Hariharan is that it acts as a bridge between people and helps in forging a relationship. This aspect comes out very strongly in Hariharan's *The Ghosts of Vasu Master* and is emphasised by Vasu, the protagonist and the storyteller: "How do we travel from one island to another? How do we ever understand another person? Or the roots that lie below the soil of his beliefs and words? Each of us has story to tell" (234).

In the novel, storytelling has also been used as an alternative and a better method of teaching. Vasu is a newly retired school teacher. His students present him a notebook at the farewell party and as he has not much to do, he begins to jot down his observations upon the nature of teaching, teacher and pupil. He also continues to teach at home but the real test of his teaching comes with the arrival of Mani, a twelve-year-old boy who has "swallowed, chewed up, spat out, outgrown his parents; four siblings; eight doctors, the last with foreign degrees and equipments; four schools and innumerable principals, teachers fellow-pupils, canes, taunts and jeers" (11). As a small child Mani was normal but the problem began only when he started to look different from other children. His head grew into a long papaya size and so when he was sent to school, not only the children even the teachers made fun of him. It was at this time that he became violent, hitting people or smashing things. Consequently, he was 'caned, shouted at, tied up'. He started speaking very little and even that generated into grunts and finally into complete silence. No school or doctor could draw him out of his reticence or help him grow in anyway. For them he was a 'complicated, intractable case'.

Mani's father brings Mani to Vasu as he has a reputation of having great patience. In the beginning, though it was not clear to Vasu whether Mani was mad or retarded or a slow learner who needed help or "a cunning precocious creature who had already mastered self-defense by feigning madness and stupidity", but even then it was clear to him that he was 'a marked child' (10). Teaching Mani becomes a real challenge for him. At first he uses conventional methods to teach Mani which assumed that "the boys could listen and learn, pay attention to what the teachers said, for forty minutes at a stretch" (13). But, Mani shows no interest in books and notebooks and cannot sit in a place for more than a few minutes at a time. All of Vasu's tricks which he had used in school fail to "halt him in his tracks and seize his attention" (14).

The growing distance between him and Mani disturbs Vasu. He explores all possible ways to build a bridge between them and finds that telling stories helps him. In due course of time he turns into a storyteller. During the course of the storytelling sessions, Vasu becomes the grey mouse and Mani, the blue bottle. Most of the stories that Vasu tells Mani are fables. The fables are a reworking of the *Buddhist Jataka Tales* and the tales of the Panchtantra, "all basically tales to serve as guides in the art of living-how to lead a good life in the worldly sense, a sensible life, a balanced life" (Hariharan, 2004: 381).

The novel traces the power of storytelling. Once the first sentence rolled off Vasu's mouth, Mani, who was always fidgeting, would sit still, completely absorbed as if "on some inward voyage", "his agitation stilled, his restlessness vanished" as if charmed by "a snake-charmer's bean pipe" (94). He was no longer indifferent or hostile either at home or with strangers and had lost "the jerky, involuntary gestures of his early days, as well as his smooth vacuous mask" (232).

In the beginning it mattered very little for Vasu what the stories were about or whether Mani understood them or not. They may or may not have added to his knowledge but Vasu's immediate purpose is achieved. Sara Cone Bryant in her *Storytelling Handbook* writes:

> Storytelling is first of all an art of entertainment, its immediate purpose is the pleasure of the listener—his pleasure, not his instruction, Especially when you are dealing with children, unless you have their attention captured all attempts to derive results from best of the story will be futile. (2004: 5)

Vasu continued to hold Mani's attention as long as he talked about animals and insects, no matter how long the story was or what it was about. Vasu's gain too was by no means less. Stories inculcated in Mani the habit to focus and concentrate which is a fundamental and indispensable habit for a child to grow. His story look was no longer 'opaque or meaningless'. Once in a while his eyes "would open to their full size, or his lips twitch as if in preparation for the near future" (187). Mani, with his eyes rested on Vasu's face while listening to stories, would have a particular look which Vasu affectionately came to think of as Mani's 'story look'. Here Vasu, comments in the capacity of storyteller, "This look was my first reward: It told me that Mani was with him, and so part of my story" (77).

Storytelling is an interactive activity. It involves both listener and narrator. In the novel Mani, though he continued to be crippled by his silence, with his "companionable, encouraging silence, and sudden quickening of something about his eyes and mouth" he became a part of the stories that Vasu told him (161).

Stories also established a happy relationship between Vasu and Mani. Mani, who was earlier hostile to Vasu, would lay a hand on his arm and lead him to his chair and "the cracks in the wall that had so far seemed impenetrable began to break down brick by brick" (233). In addition to his quiet but absorbed response to Vasu's stories, Mani took on one more role and a more active one. The images that Vasu had conveyed through his words, he re-created in the form of drawings with the pencil and paper that he had hated earlier during his school days and they were not 'mere copies but his own versions'(233). Stories, thus, enhanced his perception as well as developed his power of imagination. Vasu was elated as he could prove that Mani was not just "an idiot with an odd knack, but possessed of an intelligence which had narrowed, but he learnt to work around and despite his disabilities" (233–234). Vasu too began to supplement his tales with more real-life images in the form of drawings and "the lessons assumed the forked dimensions of theory and practice, story and drawing" (233). Mani gradually began to understand a variety of 'entangled' subjects presented as stories: "Symbol and narrative became his eyes and ears to gain a sense of the world" (222). One day Vasu made two drawings—one of a large mango and the other of a cane. He placed them before Mani who picked up the mango card, smiling at it and put it into his pocket and tore the other one. By rejecting the image of the cane, Vasu could see that Mani had "moved three steps closer to the citizenship" (148).

The stories also developed Mani's power of inference. One day Vasu told him a story in which a doe gave birth to an animal which had parts and skins of different animals. For many years the animal continued to be the favourite of all animals and came to be known as the 'Mascot of the Melting Pot' but as he grew up, the animals' attitude towards him changed. They began to avoid him and look upon him as a 'nuisance'. Then a young fox called him aside and asked him to find out who he was and decide how and where he would live. He "cannot go around like this, one week a rhino, a squirrel the next". He has to 'take sides'. He "cannot be this, that and the other, all at the same time" (80). Mascot was puzzled as he had never thought of himself as being different from other animals. When the next morning he could not tell who he was, the animals fell on him and tore him apart. When Vasu asked Mani if he liked the story, he did not reply but Vasu could see on his face "a look of bewildered reproach of betrayal like a wild animal who is relieved of a thorn in the paw only to jab it again" (81). Mani could infer that the story of Mascot was the story of his life. He too, when he was small, was loved by his parents and others but was rejected when he started looking different from other children with his papaya head.

The story which is a blending of the fabulous and the hard hitting social realism, takes up the most burning problem of India—the rise of fundamentalism—which is posing a threat to its unity. Mascot, with the skins and parts of different animals, represents India's unity in diversity. The fox 'looked pointedly' at Mascot 'whose effect was a patch work of flags' and the flag gets disintegrated 'as if the stitches holding them together had come apart' (81).

The stories that Vasu tells are fantastic but they are fantastic only in setting and have their basis in reality. Fantasy has not been used as in the world of fairy-tales where it is entirely a make-belief and constitutes the total structure. Nor is Vasu "a fairy-tale hero who sees a few sights, fights a few fights" and ends up by "wrapping up" all problems (118). Vasu Master himself comments:

> This story I am telling, I would like to believe it, I would like it to be credible with all its wants and blemishes, its missing limbs. If I don't have faith in its authenticity, if it is make-believe, I can end it the way I want to, I could wrap up

> neatly, come to terms gracefully with ancestral legacies .... And I could put word, rich polysyllables into Mani's mouth. (260)

Mani was unable to relate to reality and so Vasu presented reality in the guise of symbols and images which helped Mani "grow into something more, something closer to his silent reality rather than graft him on to romantic superfluous dimensions" (120). Though Vasu wove "magical cocoons", the cocoons were "made out of the most prosaic and ordinary materials" (161). The life stories of the animals and insects and the exaggeration and alterations of their attributes not only broke Mani's silence and indifference but they also exposed him to many occurrences and provided him with new and alternative ways of dealing with them. Mani improve and became a better person since he came to Vasu. In this connection, Jerome Singer in *Daydreaming and Fantasy* writes.

> It must be recognised that our own private experiences and images, our own symbolic alterations of the natural world or our mythological elaborations of it, are as much a part of our reality as the physically measurable stimulus field that surrounds us. Our task is not to ignore the more private set of experiences in favour of close attention to the external environment, but rather gradually to learn the conditions under which we can use both sources of stimulation for adaptive purposes. (1975: 30)

Fantasy was a way to help Mani grow out of the confines of his world and merge with the larger whole. In *The Ghosts of Vasu Master*, storytelling has also been used in the tradition of the great and eternal use of the story where the storyteller tells the story to heal the listener and also to heal himself. Vasu himself is "a timid, gentle mouse who has been taught to keep to his place—the mouse hole" and who has yet to learn the ways of the world along with Mani; the Blue Bottle (141). Fantasy provided Vasu and Mani "clues" before they "travelled further, deeper into the forest" (201). While discussing the concept of fantasy, Jerome L. Singer says further:

> Fantasy is a way by which we can explore an entire range of future possibilities. without necessarily committing ourselves through action to irrevocable consequences. Even our most fantastic daydreams may illuminate the humour in a situation or point up the incongruity between our current reality and our hopes, thereby giving us a chance to decide on a more effective approach to a life situation. In the course of fairly extensive fantasizing we may also encourage ourselves to further action in the pursuit of a particular goal. In this sense our daydreams can actually have motivational characteristics; they can encourage us to try new kinds of experiences, or at least to look for ways of reaching some compromise approach to these wishes. (1975: 118–9)

It was a kind of rehearsal for both Vasu and Mani to cope with problems without "dashing headlong against a fiery obstacle at the cost of life" (201). The stories about the lives of Vasu and Mani in the form of fables, in which Vasu was the grey mouse and Mani the blue bottle, exposed them to various incidents they might come across in their daily lives so that they could face life with courage and prudence. Also, it is in the course of fantasising that Vasu comes to recognise "the necessity of reconstruction from the dismantled parts of various beliefs, models that are his inheritance" (223), the necessity of "a new diet that does not consist entirely of old ideas, the same stale leftovers to be eaten day after day" (273).

Through the narration of fables, using Vasu Master as narrator, Hariharan subverts the present system of education which divides "theory and practice, thought and life, speculation and action" (199). Vasu's willingness to use whatever is at hand as material for the stories that eventually seems to heal the boy shows that Hariharan does not take any text or story as a closed authority, but as an open resource for the future, something that çan be rewritten according to the present day needs. In both Shashi Deshpande and Githa Hariharan storytelling is a very significant structural device. It has been used not only as a narrative strategy to reveal the complex nature of reality but also as a technique to discover and develop their theme. But, in Deshpande, storytelling is not the kind of direct subject as it is in Hariharan.

References

Abbott, Porter H. *The Cambridge Introduction to Narrative*. Cambridge: The Cambridge University Press, 2002.

Bhargava, Rajul and Shubhshree, Eds. *Of Narratives, Narrators*. Jaipur and New Delhi: Rawat Publications, 2004.

Bryant, SaraCone. *The Storytelling Handbook*. Ed. Arunima Sehgal Mukherjeee, Chandigarh: Unistar Book Pvt. Ltd., 2004.

Danta, Bijay. "Writing, Repetition and Recovery in *Small Remedies*", *Writing Difference: the Novels of Shashi Deshpande*. Ed. Chanchala K. Naik. Delhi: Pencraft International, 2005.

Deshpande, Shashi. "Lakshmi Holmstrom talks to Shashi Deshpande", *The Fiction of Shashi Deshpande*. Ed. R.S. Pathak. New Delhi: Creative Books,1998.

Fillingham, Lydia A. *Foucault*. Chennai: Orient Longman, 2000.

Garg, Mridula. "Craft of Storytelling". Creative Writing Workshop, Jaipur, 9 December, 2005.

Hariharan, Githa. "Discreet Thoughts", *Desert in Bloom*. Ed. Meenakshi Bharat. New Delhi: Pencraft International, 2004.

——. "A New take on Power". Interview with Anuradha Marwah. *Pioneer*, 7 February 1999.

——. "How and Why I Write: Githa Hariharan Answers", *Of Narratives, Narrators*. Eds. Rajul Bhargava and Shubhshree. Jaipur and New Delhi: Rawat Publications, 2004.

Jain, Jasbir. *Stairs to the Attic: The Novels of Anita Desai.* Jaipur: Printwell, 1987.

Kenan, Shlomith Rimmon. *Narrative Fiction: Contemporary Poetics.* London and New York: Routledge, 2002.

Kroeber, Karl. *Retelling/Rereading: The Fate of Storytelling in Modern Times.* New Brunswick: Rutgers University Press,1992.

Lerner, Laurence. *The Frontiers of Literature.* Oxford: Basic Blackwell,1988.

Miller, J. Hillis. "Narrative", *Critical Terms for Literary Study.* Eds. Lenntrichia & Thomas Laughlin. Chicago: University of Chicago Press, 1995.

Mukherjee, Meenakshi. "On Her Own Terms: A Reading of Shashi Deshpande's *Small Remedies*", *Desert in Bloom.* Ed. Meenakshi Bharat. Delhi: Pencraft International, 2004.

Nafisi, Azar. "Imagination as a Tool of Civic Awareness." www.rozanehmagazine.com /MarchApril/2003/anafisiMA.html.

Nair, Rukmini Bhaya. *Narrative Gravity: Conversation, Cognition, Culture.* New Delhi: OUP,2002.

——. "Narrative Evolution: In Human Cognition and Across all Cultures", *Of Narratives, Narrators.* Eds. Rajul Bhargava and Shubhshree. Jaipur and New Delhi: Rawat Publications, 2004.

Ramanujan, A.K. "Three Hundred Ramayanas", *The Collected Essays of A.K. Ramannujan.* Ed. Vinay Dharwadker. New Delhi: OUP, 2004.

Rushdie, Salman. *Midnight's Children.* London: Jonathan Cape,1981.

——. "Midnight's Children and Shame". *Kunapipi* VII, 1, 1985

Scholes, Robert and Robert Kellogg. *The Nature of Narrative.* London and New York: OUP, 1966.

Singer, Jerome L. *Day Dreaming and Fantasy.* London: George Allen and Unwin Ltd., 1975.

Waugh, Patricia. "From Metafiction", *Postmodernism and the Contemporary Fiction.* Ed. Bran Nichol. Edinburgh: EUP, 2002.

Wolfgang, Iser. "Indeterminacy and the Reader's Response to Prose Fiction", *Aspects of Narrative.* Ed. J.H. Miller. New York: Columbia University Press, 1971.

CHAPTER 6

Embedded Stories and Narrative Structure

Narrative structure may be described as the structural framework that underlies the order and manner in which a narrative is presented to a reader. Each novel, or for that matter, each work of art has a definite structure of some kind which is determined by the writer's conception of a form which he/she achieves in the contents of his/her work by the right use of technique. The relationship between structure and subject matter, or to say between form and content, is the relationship between the material nature of a work to its formal nature. The two are inseparable from each other. In "The Art of Fiction" Henry James explains the inevitable relationship between form and content by the analogy of the needle and thread. He further emphasised this point in a letter in 1913:

> I feel that in a literary work of the least complexity the very form and texture are the substance itself, and that the flesh is indetachable from the bones. (1956: 107)

The form is the *'achieved'* content. It is, as R.S. Crane also writes in "Toward a More Adequate Criticism of Poetic Structure", "a principle or complex of principles which gives to the subject-matter the power it has to affect our opinions and emotions in a certain definite way such as would not have been possible had the synthesizing principle been of a different kind" (1974: 85). This "synthesizing principle" gives an essential continuity to events, situations or actions in a work in such a manner so as to appear chronological. There is 'continuity' in a chronicle also but this continuity is achieved by ordering events in a chronological order and the relationship between events is the causal relationship. M.C. Lemon in "The Structure of Narrative" makes an important distinction between the structuring of events in a chronicle and in that of a narrative:

> A chronicle's "continuity" is merely abstract, superimposed by the purely formal rationale of the numerical ordering of dates, it is a meaningless continuity. Put more formally, the chronicle is structured in terms of this (then) that, whereas the narrative is structured in terms of this *then* that. In the narrative form, the "then" has a peculiar, distinctive significance which transforms a succession of events into a meaningful sequence … . By continuity then we do not mean the static persistence of a state of affairs but something persisting through changing state of affairs. (2001: 108–112)

A chronicle does not have an internal time sequence and its underlying structure is static. A creative artist selects out of his/her myriad impressions, feelings and thoughts and gives them a certain order and pattern. In their analysis of the nature of narrative, Robert Scholes and Robert Kellogg stress "selectivity and movement" as the two elements essential to narrative art. The two are interrelated. In chronicle, to quote them, "the lack of selectivity impedes movement and inhibits the growth of anything like a plot" (1966: 211). Emphasising the significance of the structure in a novel, James in "The Art of Fiction" maintains that each phrase, sentence or paragraph must contribute to its total effect. Virginia Woolf is also of the view that in a work of art every one of its various parts must be placed at a right place and must get "strength from another part" (1956: 248). To achieve this inner form the writer has to acquire a command over his technique. In "Technique as Discovery" Mark Schorer stresses the primacy of technique in the determination of meaning and values in fiction:

> When we speak of technique, then, we speak of nearly everything. For technique is the means by which the writer's experience, which is his subject matter, compels him to attend to it; technique is the only means he has of discovering, exploring, developing his subject, of conveying its meaning, and, finally, of evaluating it ... that the writer capable of the most exacting technical scrutiny of his subject matter, will produce works with the most satisfying content, works with thickness and resonance, works which reverberate, works with maximum meaning. (1974: 71)

According to him, technique is not merely a means of organising material but also a means of discovering and defining the meanings of that material. As such, it becomes something primary and not supplementary. As we have seen in the foregoing chapters, Shashi Deshpande and Githa Hariharan have employed the form of a story within a story in which the narrative technique becomes not only a means of arranging events but also a means of developing their theme. Each story provides meaning to the other by way of parallel or contrast. The pattern is that of 'thrust' and 'counter-thrust' in which each part modifies and is modified by the whole. Commenting on the utility of this kind of plot construction Robert Scholes and Robert Kellogg write:

> Plot, in the large sense, will always be *mythos* and always be traditional. But there are some smaller senses of the word "plot" … . Every separable element in a narrative can be said to have its own plot, its own little system of tension and resolution which contributes its bit to the general system. Not only every episode or incident but every paragraph and every system has its beginning, middle, and an end. It is in these small areas rather than in the large ones that individual achievement may be assessed … Quality of mind (as expressed in the language of characterisation, motivation, description, and commentary) not plot, is the soul of narrative. Plot is only the indispensable skeleton which, fleshed out with character and incident, provides the necessary clay into which life may be breathed. (1966: 238–9)

The loose chronological plot also allows for free and full character development without being curbed by the requirements of a tightly-knit plot. The idea of multitude and multiplicity is the central notion behind this kind of narrative pattern. Replying to a question on the role of embedded stories in *Midnight's Children,* Salman Rushdie states:

> The digressions are almost the point of the book. When I started writing, I just tried to explain one life, and it struck me more that, in order to explain this life, you had to explain a vast amount of material which surrounded it, both in space and time. (*Kunapipi*, IV, 2, 1982, 22–3)

In this connection, Githa Hariharan also states:

> I am fairly clear that in the mosaic that all these novels are, in one sense or the other, that whatever little snippets there are, in this kind of patchwork nothing is excessive. (2004: 382)

The narrative pattern employed by Githa Hariharan and Shashi Deshpande is summed up by their protagonists Vasu Master; the storyteller in *The Ghosts of Vasu Master* and Jaya; the protagonist and the writer in *That Long Silence*. Vasu says, "The frayed threads and rags in my mind were hypnotised, then drawn out into the shape of a hardy rope, all the weak, disjointed strands now linked and strengthened" (65). Similarly, Jaya says, "All that I have written—it is like one of those multi-coloured patch work quilts that Kakis made for any new baby in the family so many bits and pieces—a crazy conglomeration of shapes, sizes and colours put together" (188). The stories come to us in piecemeal, a kind of patchwork in which each "patch" is 'suggestive', and 'evocative'. The 'patches' of one life are reflected in the other. It is like picking up a stitch on the needle, each stitch adding to the whole. This narrative pattern is particularly suitable to Shashi Deshpande's view of the self as a social and cultural product embedded in relationships with others. In *Moving On*, she stresses this point:

> 'My story'—how can there be such a thing as *my* story when other people's lives are so knitted into it? I cannot pick out one stitch and say, this story is mine, take another and say, this is Baba's story, then one more and say, this is Mai's ... All our lives so entwined, so knitted together that I will never be able to separate them. (270)

Since the form in the works of both the writers draws largely on oral storytelling, it defies narrative linearity and rigid narrative cohesion in the sense that the events do not move from earlier events to the later ones. On one occasion Salman Rushdie eloquently describes how storytelling abandons linearity and goes in 'great swoops' or goes in 'spirals' or in 'loops'. The story moves forward and backward in time and sometimes 'it steps sideways', but goes back to the main story. Elaborating upon it, he writes:

> Sometimes there are Chinese boxes where there is a story inside a story inside a story inside a story, then they all come back ... So it's a very bizarre and pyrotechnical shape. And it has the appearance of being random and chaotic, it has the appearance that what is happening is anything the storyteller happens to be thinking, he just proceeds in that contingent way. It seemed to me in fact that it was very far from being random or chaotic, and that the oral narrative had developed this shape over a very long period .... (*Kunapipi*, IV, 1982: 7–8)

As the storyteller selects a vantage point in the time past or in the time present, the line between past and present is erased. In her conversation with June Gaur, emphasising the futility of segregating time into segments, Deshpande says:

> How can we divide human life into segments like past, present and future? Physically we may inhabit the present, but in our minds the past and the future are comfortably cohabiting with it. Memories and pictures of the past, dreams, hopes and the plans for the future—these are as real to us as the present. I cannot write without bringing all of them together. (*The Hindu*, Sunday, September 5, 2004)

Shashi Deshpande acknowledges in her essay "In the First Person" that the novel *That Long Silence* set the tone for all her future writings (2003: 18). The novel being "a mass of memories", there is no chronological order. Ostensibly it relates the story of Jaya, the protagonist/narrator who is an adult but the life that Jaya has spent as a child and as a young person constantly flow into the narrative through the use of flashback technique. This disrupts the temporal sequence of events and sends the narrative back to the past. Elaborating upon this technique, which "twists time" and defies the objective concept of time, Shakeel Ahmad in his book *The Theoretical Viability of the Flashback Method as a Technique of Fiction* writes:

> The result is sequential disorientation of the "genealogical imperatives" but here the disorientation does not amount to disorder although it may appear so it forges an order, a concord within a complex structure—"complexity" inhering in the aesthetic factor on account of this disorientation. This method therefore disregards cause-consequence relation by reversing the order of the narrative sequence in which the consequence displaces cause and settles itself for a starter. (1991: 29)

The narrative goes on to span a long complex past of multiple family ties. The multiple narratives constitute several sub-texts. Kusum's (Jaya's cousin) story raises the issue of gender discrimination with all its ramifications. While she was ignored by her parents with the result that she grew into a "poor, frightened, defeated woman, whose urge for destruction turned inwards", her brother Dilip boosted by his parents, always carried an aura of success around him and became a successful man though by unscrupulous means. The commonality in women's existence across generation and class is emphasised by interweaving Kusum's story with several other stories of other women. This takes the novel away from being a personal narrative and makes it a critique. The story of Kusum is, as Jasbir Jain says, "like a detonator which, as it explodes, allows us to see the faces of the witnesses in the fire that it spreads" (2003: 204). The embedding of mythological stories not only expands the narrative in terms of time and space but also fills in the gaps found in the social and cultural history of India. The folktale of the sparrow and the crow, in which the crow is burnt to death, provides a sounding board for Jaya—survival needs ruthlessness.

No story in the novel is self-contained. The story of Kamat, Jaya's friend whose death has taken place outside the narrative time of the novel and who is resurrected through memory, also serves several purposes. In the first place, it counters Jaya's state of utter despair and helplessness and reassures her about a self which can be expressed in writing. This infuses into her a sense of independence and confidence which helps her in her journey towards self actualisation. But what is significant is that Jaya's self-realisation comes with Kamat's death. His death, Deshpande says "brings a whole process of defining [Jaya] to a decisive point. If the relationship had gone on, this point of realisation would never have come" (1995: 23). The story also reflects how this kind of relationship in Indian society is looked upon with suspicion and disapproval and obstructs the free communication between man and woman. Diaries, which Jaya has written in the past, are also crucial to the development of the plot. They lead her to confession and self-realisation. The 'silence' of the title is a recurring design used as both the oppressor's infliction and a woman's strategy.

What is remarkable about the novel is also the seamlessness with which intense spillage of personal emotions merges a concern with creativity and the role of the artist, a theme which is explored more intensively in *Small Remedies*, "if you want to be a saint, if you want to love the whole world, you've got to stop loving individual human beings first. ...There's just no other way of being a saint. Or a painter. A writer" (1). The creative artist has to transcend his or her personal feelings in order to reach out to wider territories of experiences.

One of the recurring themes in Deshpande is loss, loss through death. But most such incidents have usually been placed outside the narrative frameworks of the novels. Since deaths are in immediate relationships to the protagonists/narrators, the long-term consequences of these deaths constantly flow into the narrative The stories of such already over incidents come to us not through any sequentially realistic narration, but in a fluid movement that follows the fragmented subjectivities of the characters' minds. The constant movement between the characters' external world on the one hand and the internal, fragmented life of the mind and its fluid movements on the other constitutes one of the major structural devices. The placing of the narrative outside the frameworks of the novels is not only temporal but also spatial as in *The Binding Vine* where the incident of Kalpana's rape has been placed outside the narrative frame, even though it happens within the ambit of the narrative present. Located much farther back in the past, the story of Mira's life, Urmi's (the protagonist) long-dead mother-in-law, comes to life only through the diaries and the poems Mira has left behind. The story of Mira is the story of a woman whose husband claims her body against her will. Documents play an important role in almost all of Deshpande's novels. The issue of marital rape surfaces through the unravelling of Mira's diaries which goes on to take up the issue of a woman's right to her body. Commenting on this Jasbir Jain writes:

> By introducing the concept of marital rape, Deshpande not only anticipates the surfacing of this issue in feminist discourse in India but also reflects upon feminist history in the Indian context and the rights of a wife visa-a-vis the husband. The notion of romantic love as an obsessive imposition on the woman is also put forth as representing an anti-romantic instance, a construction of the idea of love necessarily being a fulfilment. (2004: 211)

Mira's life-story dissects the notion of romantic love and comments on the appropriation of womens' bodies through marriage. The two rapes—within and outside marriage—seen from different class background and different generations, indicate larger patterns of class and gender oppression. The incident of Kalpana's rape, "Mira's narrative", as Jasbir Jain observes, "when contrasted with Urmi's, reflects the social change that has come about but when compared with Kalpana's, it heightens class difference where sex, sexuality and marriage are concerned" (2003: 274). The theme of the sexual domination of women's bodies dealt with in *The Dark Holds No Terrors* finds a broader, more intense space in *The Binding Vine*. Mira's narrative turns out to be a discussion on literature, on women's writing and the reconstruction of women's lives through writing also when Priti, a budding star in the novel, insists on giving a "woman's vision" to Mira's life and poems and Urmi declines to go for an academic dissection of Mira's writing, geared towards a feminist issue. The question as to why a woman's communion with herself must be made public or why her story must be recovered and represented is asked by Vanna, "It all happened so long ago. Why do you need to rake it up? Why? What do you want?" (173).

In *The Binding Vine* there are stories of other women which open out several other issues such as the girl child and society, marriage in Indian society, woman and household chores, woman's career and family, relationship between mother and daughter and so on. The novel is multi-layered. According to Mrinalini Sebastian, the book can be read as a narrative of feminism, a narrative suggesting the restructuring of the society, or "a narrative demanding radical questioning—is also a narrative which is built upon silence" (2000: 165). The novel is divided into four parts, each part preceded by short poetical extracts from the poems by Mira. Part one which deals with Urmi's childhood, her grandparents and also about Mira's life takes the narrative back in the past Part two brings the narrative back in the present, and focuses on Kalpana, her rape and consequently her going into coma. Part three expands on the issue of rape. Part four makes the reader ponder over the predicament of human existence and gives a metaphysical dimension to the book which extends the horizon of the narrative structure.

Small Remedies is divided into two parts, prefaced by a prologue. At its simplest level, it tells the story of Madhu but several stories and strands have been woven into it. Madhu's attempt to write the biography of Savitribai, a living person and an artist problematises the relationship between fiction and reality, and delineates the role of language in our attempts to construct our own realities. It also reinforces the idea that while writing, there cannot be progression in a linear manner because life is "fluid, inchoate and incomplete". So this novel is as much about the creative process as it is about the characters inhabiting the fictional world. The narrative might have been filtered through the voice of Madhu but it refuses to be monologic. There is the voice of Savitribai, giving her own version of her life as a singer, Hasina "modifying" it by giving her version of Ghulam Saab's story and his role in Bai's life, Munni with her "stubborn adherence to her own truth" and so on.

The narrative structure of *Small Remedies* works through echoes and reflections. There is a lot that is common to both Madhu and Bai. Bai's daughter Munni was Madhu's childhood friend and like her son Aditya, she too was killed in the same bomb blast. But while Madhu has not been able to come out of this shock and whom early motherhood had absorbed to the extinct of self-denial, Bai acknowledges neither Munni as her daughter nor Madhu as Munni's friend. Madhu's attempt to unmask the mother behind the successful artist in Bai is really an attempt to understand her own self. Madhu's journey into her own past, starting from the days when Bai was her neighbour to the day she lost her son, ends up in the writing of her own biography within the biography of Savitribai. The desperate search for meaning, the effort to find a sense of one's identity and one's relationship to the world outside are also some of the issues which have been explored through the stories of Savitribai and Leela who realise their potential by exercising their choices as individuals.

Like *Small Remedies,* Hariharan's *The Thousand Faces of Night* is also a configuration of diverse discourses and elements. On the surface, it is the story of Devi, a young educated girl coping with a failed marriage but she is linked with the second generation through her mother Sita and also with the first through her grandmother and Mayamma, the old family retainer. Myths and folklore intersect to provide a framework to Devi's story. What is remarkable about the novel is Devi's performing the creative role of the 'reader' to the other stories which lends a subversive dimension to it.

The novel has three main divisions, sub-divided into chapters. The narrative goes back in time as Devi relives the days of her childhood spent in her grandmother's house and the mythological stories told to her by the grandmother. She reconstructs the life of her mother Sita in the light of the stories that she has 'received'. This makes the narrative move back and forth all the time between past and present, between incidents and memories. The story of Parvatiamma, Devi's mother-in-law whom she had never seen, is revealed to her in pieces by her father-in-law and her husband Mahesh and also by Mayamma. Devi recreates the story from the conflicting versions received about her. She also listens to Mayamma's story of suffering and experiences and finds traces of it in her own life. Though the three women Sita, Devi and Mayamma belong to three different generations, they are linked through commonality of their experience. Their stories go on linking women's lives and struggles across generations and class. The world of prosaic reality has been juxtaposed with the idyllic world. The story of the romantic love of Nala and Damayanti and their 'swayamvara', which Devi heard in her childhood, has been placed against her being exhibited as a 'commodity'.

The rendering of conflicting discourses and tradition in the novel is quite intriguing. On the one hand, there are Baba's (Devi's father-in-law) stories, full of examples of virtuous and chaste women inspiring their husbands along the path of 'dharma' by their self-denial and servitude, defining the limits of 'womanhood', on the other hand, are the grandmother's stories of dazzling gods and goddesses vested with 'the subterranean possibilities of womanhood'. The cross currents of these conflicting discourses let the different choices speak for themselves, the choice to conform or to break free.

The novel thus "moves through a number of voices, predominantly that of women and evolves through a concentric framework of storytelling, containing stories embedded within stories, the real and the mythical colliding and colluding, reflecting and intersecting with each other" (Mukhopadhyay, 2005: 161). The story line, though simple, reaches out in multiple directions through the appropriation and reworking of myth and folklore.

A Matter of Time marks a significant departure from the interiority and silences of earlier works. The novel is divided into three sections prefaced by epigraphs from the *Upanishads* which form an integral part of the narrative structure and contribute to the articulation of meaning in multiple ways. Part I "The House" begins with a line from the *Brhad-aranyaka Upanishad*: "Maitreyi," said Yagnavalkya, "verily I am about to go forth from this state (of householder)." It refers to the movement towards renunciation and relates to Gopal who deserts his family, abdicating the household responsibility and through this Deshpande works out an entire patriarchal structure. Does society sanction this kind of freedom to a woman? Gopal justifies his act: "for a woman from the moment she is pregnant, there is an overriding reason for living, a justification for life that is loudly and emphatically true. A man has to search for it, always and for ever" (68). This reflects, as Usha Bande points out, patriarchal ideology that a woman is fulfilled though childbirth and therefore she does not have existential problems (2005: 194). The epigraph to part II "The Family", again from the *Brhad-aranyaka Upanishad*:

"whatever wrong has been done by him, his son frees him from it all; therefore he is called a son. By his son a father stands firm in this world" (91) makes central the import of a son. The significance of a son in the religious, cultural and social context in India has endured from ancient times to the present. The novel is replete with references to sons and significantly, towards the end of the novel, Aru cries out when Kalyani collapses at the death of her husband and daughter, "Amma, I'm here. I'm your daughter, Amma, I'm your son" (233). Part III "The River" begins with an epigraph from the *Katha-Upanishad* where Yama asks Nachiketa not to probe the mystery of death: "Whatever desires are hard to attain in this world of mortals, ask for all those desires at thy will. O Nachiketa, (pray) ask not about death" (181). The section emphasises the inevitability of death and the flow of life.

The three sections are further divided into chapters which alternate between the first and the third person. This alternative voice not only makes for double perspective, it enables the author to tell her story with hindsight. The third person is used to write the story of Sumi and other characters. The first person narration is used to bring out the thoughts and actions of Gopal in the form of self-reflections and interior monologues. The narrative continuity is often broken through the juxtaposition of the exterior and the interior worlds of the characters. Many a times the two are oppositional to each other and create a second level of narrative as does, for example, Kalyani's story. Kalyani and her husband have not spoken to each other for thirty years. Aunt Premi tells Aru that after Kalyani's son, who was abnormal, went missing, Shripati has withdrawn himself into complete silence. Aru and her sister often wondered if Kalyani had lost the son deliberately since he was very difficult to manage. Interestingly enough, later in the novel, we are led to believe this version of the story. We are given 'Sumi's vision of Kalyani' in which Kalyani is slapping herself in an act of violent self-retribution

(184). This altogether changes our view of the Shripati-Kalyani story. The stories thus, altered by the revelations and the readers' insights into the characters' thoughts or memories, emphasise the elusive and complex nature of reality.

Though the novel has a failed marriage at its centre, the plot does not simply revolve around what happens when a man deserts his family. It addresses some important issues: Why is it that a man walks out on his family? Is it the saint in him that makes him do so or is it an abdication of responsibility? The metaphysical question of the ultimate truth of human life and the persistent search for meaning in existence, raised through the story of Sumi and Gopal, runs as an undercurrent in the novel.

A number of sub-narratives are woven into the fabric of the novel. These sub-narratives act as decentralising factors with no individual protagonist being the sole concern of the story. The story of the princess, which Sumi recalls, and which later becomes the subject matter of her play, reflects the survival strategy adopted by women when they know that their desire will not materialise. The princess loves the gardener's son and she knows that her father would object to it. She tells her father that she would marry only that man who could identify the plant she feeds with rice and curd, knowing fully well that the gardener's son sees her everyday feeding it with rice and curd. Her wish is fulfilled. This story forms the subtext of how promises have been used as weapons. Sumi is reminded how Kaikeyi succeeded in sending Ram into exile because of the promise that Dashrath had made to her long ago. From there, Sumi goes on to reflect on the futility of making promises for the future: "things change with time, people change, circumstances change, nothing is constant" (157). The concept of 'honour' is also dissected. Dashrath fulfilled his promise for the sake of his honour and Sumi reflects "was honour worth all the tragedy that followed?" (157)

Documents are again part of the narrative structure in *A Matter of Time* as they are in the form of diaries in *That Long Silence* and *The Binding Vine.* Kalyani shows Gopal her family document which has a history behind it. As Gopal goes through the documents, he can see how Vithalrao, the writer of the history, blinded by family loyalty and pride, has left gaps and inconsistencies in it. This takes the narrative further to a questioning of past, of history and memory: "There are alterations and deletions but we pretend they are not there as there are certain things which we want to forget and certain things and beliefs we want to live with and so we ignore them" (199). What Shashi Deshpande is emphasising here is that past is constructed in multiple ways, yet we cannot sever our relationship with the past. There is this very complex relationship with the past.

Many a time the structure is circular in the novels of Deshpande. *Roots and Shadows* has a prologue, followed by eleven chapters, which begins with the day before Mini's wedding and the novel ends with Indu deciding to pay for her wedding. The prologue may well pass off as an epilogue. The narrative is thus circular in structure. Both Mrinalini Sebastian and Adele King draw attention to the circularity of structure in Deshpande which follows cyclical concept of time. This is more clearly seen in *A Matter of Time* where Sumi visits her husband one year after he has left her and comments:

> Living with Amma, I have begun to see it differently. A *year* I mean. For her it is just not a chunk that gets cut off and then it is over. No it is all mixed with the seasons, flowers and fruits. It is a cycle. Nothing is over, things keep coming back over and over again, they are all connected. (219)

This approach to the concept of time accounts for the open-endedness as well as lack of sequential description in the novels of Shashi Deshpande.

Hariharan's *The Ghosts of Vasu Master* has three epigraphs prefaced to the work which define and extend the theme of the novel. The first one is from Charaka and goes like this: "The entire world is a teacher to the intelligent and foe to the unintelligent." This foregrounds the theme of the novel. The second from Shakespeare emphasises the limitation of human knowledge: "We cannot all be masters, nor all masters cannot be truly followed". The third is from Gandhi where he admits, "I have nothing new to teach the world." This emphasises the humbleness that is required on the part of a teacher and also the necessity of reorienting the already existing knowledge according to time and the individual requirement.

The story begins with the simple life of a retired school teacher but the novel is not about the lonely life of a retired school teacher. Vasu Master revisits the past and examines his legacy in an attempt to understand the present. The novel addresses some larger questions: Does the present education system, through its classroom teaching and examination, prepare the student for the life that he is going to encounter? Does anything new or organic grow with cramming? A related question that is raised is: how does one define and measure intelligence? Is it to be defined and measured by the ability to give answers that the teachers want? Or is it to be measured by the child's individual ability? Two strands—the healing of the mind and the healing of the body are interwoven and are seen as interdependent. A teacher has to be a psychologist, a pedagogue, and also a mother. Structured through memories, dreams and fantasies, the narrative dismantles various inherited ideas, beliefs and models.

The novel bears a remarkable affinity to the *Panchtantra* in its general spirit, its reiteration of certain themes and motifs and its structure. Like the *Panchtantra,* it employs the device of the chain story throughout, interwoven with reflections on education, alternative methods of teaching, ancient Indian education, Indian healing systems and healing in general. The teachings of the *Panchtantra* are illustrated in a number of stories dealing both with human beings and animals. Some of these are 'The Crow and the Mouse', 'The Crow and the Great Cobra'. Story after story follows and the narrative structure becomes multi-dimensional. The story "The Mascot of the Melting Pot" takes up the rise of fundamentalism which has posed a challenge to the idea of unity in diversity, an idea long cherished in the country. The novel explores the human condition and the underlying principles of all human condition.

Thus, we see that in the novels of both Shashi Deshpande and Githa Hariharan, to begin with, there is one story of one individual but several dimensions are added on to it by fusing the individual voices with other voices. The narrative grows like 'a banyan tree', that is to say, "it sprouts, and grows, and spreads and drops down branches that become trunks and intertwine with other branches. Sometimes the main trunk dies, and the structure is held up by the supporting trunks ... . But then it's also like the Ganges in its upper, middle and lower courses—including the delta of course" (Vikram Seth, *A Suitable Boy*, 483). The narrative expands both in terms of time and space by means of its 'branches', making the narrative structure more complex and yet integrated.

References

Ahmad, Shakeel. *The Theoretical Viability of the Flashback Method as a Technique of Fiction*. Gaya: New Concept Publications, 1991.

Bande, Usha. "Resistance and Reconciliation: Shashi Deshpande's *A Matter of Time* and *Small Remedies*", *Writing Difference: The Novels of*

Shashi Deshpande. Ed. Chanchala K. Naik. New Delhi: Pencraft International, 2005.

Crane, R.S. "Toward a More Adequate Criticism of Poetic Structure", *Twentieth Century Criticism*. Ed. William J. Handy and Max Westbrook. New Delhi: Light and Life Publishers, 1974.

Deshpande, Shashi. "In Conversation with June Gaur". *The Hindu*, September 5, 2004.

——. "In the First Person", *Writing from the Margin and Other Essays*. New Delhi: Viking, 2003.

Edel, Leon, ed. *The Selected Letters of Henry James*. New York: Farrar, Straus & Cudahy, 1956.

Jain, Jasbir. *Gendered Realities: Human Spaces: The Novels of Shashi Deshpande*. Jaipur and Delhi: Rawat Publications, 2003.

——. "Shashi Deshpande", *A Companion to Indian Fiction in English*. Ed. Pier Piciucco. Atlantic Publishers: New Delhi: 2004.

James, Henry. "The Art of Fiction", *The House of Fiction*. Ed. Leon Edel. London: Mercury Books, 1962.

Lemon, M.C. "The Structure of Narrative", *The History and Narrative Reader*. Ed. Geoffrey Roberts. London and New York: Routledge, 2001.

Mukhopadhyay, Arpita Chattaraj. "*The Thousand Faces of Night*: A 'Story' of 'Storytelling", *Studies in Women Writers in English*. Eds. Mohit K. Ray and Rama Kundu. New Delhi: Atlantic, 2005.

Chaudhary, Romita. "Interview with Shashi Deshpande". *World Literature Written in English* 34: 2,1995.

Rushdie, Salman. "Midnight's Children and Shame". *Kunapipi* IV, 2, 1982.

Scholes, Robert, and Robert, Kellogg. *The Nature of Narrative*. London: OUP, 1966.

Schorer, Mark. "Technique as Discovery", *Twentieth Century Criticism*. Ed. William J Handy and Max Westbrook. New Delhi: Light and Life Publishers, 1974.

Sebastian, Mrinalini. *The Novels of Shashi Deshpande in Postcolonial Arguments*. New Delhi: Prestige, 2000.

Seth, Vikram. *A Suitable Boy*. Delhi: Penguin India, 1992.

Woolf, Virginia. *A Writer's Diary*. Ed. Leonard Woolf. London: The Hogarth Press,1956.

CHAPTER 7

Conclusion

The master storytellers Shashi Deshpande and Githa Hariharan, as discussed in the foregoing chapters, weave in a fine tapestry, different lives and events drawn together like the strands of a warp and a weft. The realities of life are expressed in a maze of intertwined stories where one complements, contradicts, reflects and refracts the other. One has to take them together to make sense of life and catch a glimpse of the complex whole. They dwell upon a central idea and deal with it in the various threads of their plot and story, a pattern about which Virginia Woolf writes in her diary: "… I saw the form of a novel. It is to be first the statement of the theme: then the restatement: and so on: repeating the same story: singling out this and then that, until the central idea is stated" (1953: 287). Though the central structuring principle is a kind of repetition, it is not just the recurrence of the same static elements. Rather it is the process by which various strands (from individual images and characters to entire situations and stories) reappear in an intricate web of relationship and multiple signification. The narrative movement is both centrifugal as the narrative moves away from the main story and a centripetal one as it moves towards accretion through cumulative repetition around a singular structural centre.

Both the writers have embraced India's cultural heritage, texts like the *Panchtantra,* the *Ramayana,* the *Mahabharata,* the storytelling traditions and have interwoven lives past and present, personal and political in the story within a story framework. Mythological stories embedded in their narratives not only provide the cultural matrix, they also help to shape the characters, to view their actions and to subvert received notions of traditions and accepted behaviour patterns. Self—seen both as a personal and a cultural construct—there is a constant questioning of cultural inheritance and a reframing of it through a process of conflict. Persistent struggle against tradition budges the margins of the boundaries. T.S. Eliot's theory of tradition and innovation bears a remarkable relevance to the works of these writers. In them we find that while the present works through the past, the present at the same time reworks the past. The juxtaposition of the past and the present opens out the multiplicities and ambivalences which are present in the tradition. By revisiting the *Mahabharata* and the *Ramayana,* these writers have laid bare hitherto marginalised, unheard voices. *That Long Silence* and *The Thousand Faces of Night* deal with alternatives when older paradigms are no more relevant. Both the novels give a perspective that is sociologically modern and historically a reassessment of the past and the way it bears down.

The answer to the question whether or not Shashi Deshpande and Githa Hariharan belong to the school of realism is both 'yes' and 'no'. One can see that though both the writers work through actual life situations (Hariharan's *When Dreams*

Travel being an exception) and the characters are individualised versions of recognisable social types, yet their works can be placed only broadly within the framework of 'realism'. "The narrative structure, as Jasbir Jain also observes, "works at two levels; the first is identified in realistic terms—education, economic independence, recognition of self-worth and acceptance of desire. They are all necessary routes to subjecthood. The second structure works through narrative terms-memory, myth and female communities" (2003: 275). Structured through interrupted time sequences, fragmented narrations, memories, dreams, fantasies, and also surrealistic visions and epiphanies, the narratives go on to incorporate elements of surrealism. Memory being selective and subjective, the past is remembered differently by different people. Various versions of truth emerge and the picture of the past continues to shift. The gap between what one experiences and what one remembers also destabilises reality.

Just as memory dominates the narrative structure so does fantasy which manifests itself at different levels in different ways. But the use of fantasy does not in any way deny reality and at some point coalesces with the normative, commonly accepted world view. Sometimes it is used to create an alternative reality or to contrast the two or more visions of reality. In *When Dreams Travel* fantasy and reality have been so deftly woven that it blurs the demarcating line between the two. Another method employed to comment on the complex nature of reality in the works of Shashi Deshpande and Githa Hariharan, more in Deshpande, is the use of stream of consciousness technique. This technique, described by Erich Auerbach as "a method which dissolves reality into multiple and multivalent reflections of consciousness", reveals the 'other' voice of the characters (cited in Scholes and Kellogg, 1976: 203). This creates a second level of narrative within the larger one and a double perspective. Each informs the other into a mosaic of complex narrative pattern. Fusion of hard hitting social realism with the internal, fragmented life of the mind and its fluid movements through uncharted territories constitutes one of the most powerful structural elements of their fictional world.

Storytelling being an important tool in the writings of these two writers, it not only provides space for the narration of the same event by different people but also allows for contradictory views to emerge as the events are retold or recalled. The stories are built on the principle of interacting structures of 'repetition, elaboration and variation'. The narrative structure in this way works through contradictions, inversions and multiple views affecting and animating one another. Storytelling has also enabled these two writers to frequently change their axis in both time and space as the storyteller selects a vantage point in the time past or in the time present. Thus, past, present and future achieve simultaneity and are at once viewed from various perspectives.

In addition to this, storytelling has been used as a subject. *The Ghosts of Vasu Master* explores the various functions that storytelling performs—the therapeutic use, as a mode of instruction and learning and also as a vehicle to build connections for us with our surroundings. Vasu learns what it is to teach and heal by telling stories to Mani, a mute child. *When Dreams Travel* looks quite directly at the mutability of stories. In the novel, the same story mutates in all kinds of ways to look at love, power and sexuality from different points. Since storytelling also involves an expression of the suppressed feelings, it also enables all the protagonists to come out of their shells, analyse themselves and visualise the possibility of a new life. The telling of stories in *The Thousand Faces of Night*, especially by women, creates an alternative, fictional world and aims at negotiating reality. In *That Long Silence* also, mythological stories help Jaya learn what is expected from her as a woman and how she can twist and turn these expectations to survive. Storytelling also leads to the development of the characters. For example, in *The Ghosts of Vasu Master* stories in the form of fable and allegory teach both Mani and Vasu practical wisdom enabling them to meet the challenges of life.

The narrative structure consists of a pattern in which there are stories within stories and the main story serves as a knot that holds the parts together. Though the embedded stories come to us in bits and pieces yet a certain continuity is maintained as each story flows into the other. Characters from one story reappear in another but never in the state we have known, for as the narrative progresses, time flows, perspectives shift and relationships evolve, giving us disturbing insights into the supposedly humdrum lives of ordinary people. Thus, the characters are formulated not out of accumulative processes but as a result of revisions and retractions. Even if the story is filtered through the consciousness of a central character, the narrator is not a recorder or a recounter but an investigator who examines the past with an eye toward separating out reality from myth and who also presents conflicting versions in his/her search for the truth. However, most of the novels work through multiple consciousnesses as there is narration within narration. In almost all the novels, the voices and memories of the sub-narrators consistently surface and add a new perception to each story. The co-presence of several voices which many a times are conflictual and contradictory reminds one of Mikhail Bakhtin's words about Dostoevsky's heroes "Every thought senses itself to be from the very beginning a *rejoinder* in an unfinished dialogue. Such thought is not impelled towards a well rounded, finalised, systematically monologic whole. It lives a tense life on the borders of someone else's consciousness" (cited in Dharwadker, 2004: 447). The narratives are thus dominantly dialogic, sidestepping the main protagonist and opening out the discourse to several voices.

As we have seen, the narrative structure also consists of a pattern in which almost each novel begins with some kind of upheaval in the lives of the protagonists. These upheavels trigger off past memories and also lead to the unravelling of the unconscious as a result of which some larger questions emerge which transcend their immediate contexts and private lives spill into the larger patterns or upheavals of the public domain. Intertextual references from different cultures echo in multiple ways and create a whole universe of meaning. They frequently refer not only to the *Ramayana*, the *Mahabharata* and the *Upanishads* but also to writers from the west. Some of the visible passages cited are from the Brontes, Dickens, T.S. Eliot, Jane Austen, Faulkner and Shakespeare and thus they have embraced different traditions of the oral and written cultures.

The remarkable way in which the embedded stories have expanded the narrative structure both in terms of time and space gives an extra dimension to the novels. Most of the novels of these writers begin with a small space—say the space of a woman, a child, or an old man, but then gradually this small space turns out to be spacious. For example the novel *The Ghosts of Vasu Master* (Hariharan) is located in a small town in the south of India and begins with the simple life of a school maste, Vasu but the story is not about the lonely life of a retired teacher. By means of embedded stories, the narrative opens out in multiple ways. Vasu's attempt to educate Mani through storytelling which teaches the art of living drifts into a critiquing of the current system of education which lays too much emphasis on cramming and does not prepare one to encounter human life. Similarly, *The Thousand Faces of Night* and *That Long Silence* begin with the personal stories of Devi and Jaya, but in both the cultural myths extend the space that provides opportunity for effecting a positive reconstruction of the past. *In Times of Siege*, which looks into the ugliness of rising fundamentalism, the theme which finds echoes in *Small Remedies*, holds up a mirror to the world at large, convincing us about the truth value in the writers' observations about society, about history and politics, convincing in their feminist and other ideological stances.

To conclude, both the writers have addressed several social issues of contemporary India but within earshot of their protagonists' small personal voices, concealing narratives within narratives and yet remaining blindingly clear in all their exposition of private and public lives. To quote Githa Hariharan the narrative structure is like, "a series of Chinese boxes where we open one box to find another and still another till the narrative has penetrated to the smallest box, the kernel of the matter" (2004: 380). The narratives constructed are like Chinese boxes, the embedded stories are not just additional but important and integral both in terms of form and content. Haroun in *Haroun and the Sea of Stories* employs a juggling metaphor to describe the dynamics of storytelling which can be aptly applied to these two writers: "I always thought storytelling was like juggling … . You keep a lot of different tales in the air and juggle them up and down, and if you are good you don't drop any. So may be juggling is a kind of storytelling too" (1990:109). In their works all the disparate stories interlock and come together into an integrated pattern. The careful layering of various stories has made their works wide and rich in range and complex in structure.

References

Hariharan, Githa. "How and Why I Write: Githa Hariharan Answers", *Of Narratives and Narrators*. Eds. Rajul Bhargava and Shubhshree. New Delhi and Jaipur: Rawat Publications, 2004.

Jain, Jasbir. *Gendered Realities, Human Spaces: The Writing of Shashi Deshpande*. New Delhi and Jaipur: Rawat Publications, 2003.

Ramanujan, A.K. "Three Hundred *Ramayanas*: Five Examples and Three Thoughts on Translation", *The Collected Essays of A.K. Ramanujan*. Ed. Vinay Dharwadker. New Delhi: OUP, 2004.

Rushdie, Salman. *Haroun and the Sea of Stories*. London: Granta Books, 1990.

Scholes, Robert and Robert Kellogg. *The Nature of Narrative*. New York: Oxford University Press, 1966.

Woolf, Leonard, ed. *A Writer's Diary*. London: The Hogarth Press, 1953.

Bibliography

Primary Sources

Shashi Deshpande

Fiction

A Matter of Time. New Delhi: Penguin, 1996.

Collected Short Stories. Vol. I, New Delhi: Penguin, 2003.

Come Up and Be Dead. New Delhi: Vikas Publishing House, 1983.

If I Die Today. New Delhi: Tarang Paperbacks, Vikas Publishing House, 1982.

In the Country of Deceit. Penguin,2009

It was Dark. Calcutta: Writers Workshop, 1986.

Moving On. New Delhi: Penguin, 2004.

Roots and Shadows. Hyderabad: Sangam Books, Orient Longman Ltd. 1983.

Small Remedies. New Delhi: Viking, Penguin, 2000.

That Long Silence. (F.P. Virago, 1988) New Delhi: Penguin, 1989.

The Binding Vine. New Delhi: Penguin, 1993.

The Dark Holds No Terrors. (F.P. Vikas, 1980) New Delhi: Penguin,1990.

The Legacy. Calcutta: Writers Workshop, 1978.

The Miracle and Other Stories. Calcutta: Writers Workshop, 1986.

The Stone Women and Other Stories. Calcutta: Writers Workshop, 2000.

Non-Fiction

"No Woman is an Island". *The Sunday Times of India*, May 10, 1992.

"Of Concerns, Of Anxieties". *Women in Indo-Anglian Fiction: Tradition and Modernity*. Ed. Naresh K. Jain. New Delhi: Manohar Publications, 1998.

"On the Writing of a Novel". *Indian Women Novelists*. Ed.R.K Dhawan. New Delhi: Prestige, 1991.

"On Women's Writing". *Women in Women's Writing*. Ed. T. Ashok Rani. Tirupati: Sri Padmavati Mahila Visvavidyalam, 1995.

"The Dilemma of a Woman Writer". *The Fiction of Shashi Deshpande*. Ed. R.S. Pathak. New Delhi: Creative Books, 1998.

"The Great Tradition?" *Literature Alive*, Vol. 4 and 5, February 1992.

"Writing and Activism". *Writing Difference: Novels of Shashi Deshpande*. Ed. Chanchala K. Naik. New Delhi: Pencraft International, 2005.

Writing from the Margin and Other Essays. New Delhi: Viking, 2003.

Interviews

"A Woman's World ... All the Way" with Vanmala Vishwanatha, *The Fiction of Shashi Deshpande*. Ed. R.S. Pathak. New Delhi: Creative Books, 1998.

"Denying the Otherness" with Geetha Gangadharan, *The Fiction of Shashi Deshpande*. Ed. R.S. Pathak. New Delhi: Creative Books, 1998.

"In Conversation with Shashi Deshpande", Vimala Rama Rao, *The Fiction of Shashi Deshpande*. Ed. R.S. Pathak. New Delhi: Creative Books, 1998.

"In Conversation with Shashi Deshpande", Gita Viswanath, *Writing Difference: The Novels of Shashi Deshpande*. Ed. Chanchala K. Naik. New Delhi: Pencraft, 2005.

"In Conversation with Shashi Deshpande", June Gaur, *The Hindu*, September 5, 2004.

"Interview with Shashi Deshpande", Sue Dickman. *Ariel* Vol. 29, No. 1, January 1998.

"Shashi Deshpande talks to Lakshmi Holmstrom", *The Fiction of Shashi Deshpande*. New Delhi: Creative Books,1998.

"There is No Looking Back" with M.D. Riti, *The Fiction of Shashi Deshpande*. Ed. R.S. Pathak. New Delhi: Creative Books, 1998.

Githa Hariharan

Fiction

Art of Dying and Other Stories. New Delhi: Penguin Books, 1993.

Fugitive Histories. New Delhi: Penguin Books, 2009.

In Times of Siege. New York: Pantheon Books, 2003.

The Ghosts of Vasu Master. New Delhi: Penguin Books, 1994.

The Thousand Faces of Night. London: Women's Press, 1996.

The Winning Team. New Delhi: Rupa & Company, 2004.

When Dreams Travel. London: Picador, 1999.

Non-Fiction

"Discreet Thoughts", *Desert in Bloom*. Ed. Meenakshi Bharat. New Delhi: Pencraft International, 2004.

"In Times of Siege: Shrinking Spaces in Times of Globalization", *Littcrit*, Vol. 31, No. 1, June 2005.

"New Voices: New Challenges", *Littcrit*, Vol. 30, No. 1, June 2004.

Interviews

"A New Take on Power" with Anuradha Marwah Roy, *The Pioneer*, February 7, 1999.

"A Conversation with Arnab Chakladar". May 5, 2006 <http://www. anothersubcontinent.com/gh1.html.

"Close to the Bone" with Kala Krishnan Ramesh, *The Hindu*, April 24, 2003.

"Mark her Words" with Debbie Rodgers, *The Deccan Herald*, May 3, 2003.

"My Voice Seems Right for Medley" with Rukmini Bhaya Nair, *The Times of India*, January 17, 1999.

"Plea for Pluralism" with Gouri Ramnarayan, *The Hindu*, April 24, 2003.

"Resisting Regimentation" with Anuradha Roy, *The Hindu* March 2, 2003.

"Stage Presence" with Sumithra Thangavelu, *The Indian Express*, May 6, 2003.

"Telling it like it is" with Ella Dutta, *The Hindusan Times*, February 23, 2003.

"The Cerebral Erotica was Fun" with Urvashi Butalia, *Outlook*, February 1, 1999.

"Touched by the Times" with Utpal Bhojpuri, *The Deccan Herald*, April 27, 2003.

Secondary Sources

Abbott, H. Porter. *The Cambridge Introduction to Narrative*. Cambridge: The Cambridge University Press, 2002.

Abrams, A.H. *A Glossary of Literary Terms*. New Delhi: Macmillan, 2001.

Adam, Ian and Helen Tiflin, eds. *Past the Last Post: Theorizing Post-Colonialism and Post-Modernism*. New York: Harvester Wheatsheaf, 1991.

Agarwal, R.S. *Indian Writing in English: A Critical Study*. New Delhi: Atlantic Publishers, 2003.

Ahmad, Aijaz. *In Theory: Classes, Nations, Literatures*. Delhi: OUP, 1992.

Ahmad, Shakeel. *The Theoretical Viability of the Flashback as a Technique of Fiction*. Gaya: New Concept Publications, 1991.

Ahmed, Hena Zafar. *Post-National Feminism in Third Women's Literature*. Boston: University of Massachusetts, 1996.

Albrow, Martin. *Globalisation: Myths and Realities*. London: Roehampton Institute, 1994.

Allen, Walter, ed. *Writers on Writing*. London: Phoenix House, 1948.

——. *Reading a Novel*. London: Phoenix House, 1963.

Appachana, Anjana. *Incantations and Other Stories*. New Delhi: Penguin, 1991.

Ashcroft, Gareth Griffiths and Helen Tifflin. *Key Concepts in Postcolonial Studies*. London: Routledge, 1995.

Bai, Kalle Meera. *Women's Voices: The Novels of Indian Women Writers*. New Delhi: Prestige, 1996.

Bala, Suman, ed. *Women in the Novels of Shashi Deshpande*. New Delhi: Khosla Publishing House, 2001.

Bande, Usha, "Tolerance of Female Altrusim: A Study of Shashi Deshpande's *A Matter of Time*". *Language Forum*, Vol. XXIV, Nos. 1–2, January-December 1998.

——, ed. *Mothers and Mother Figures in Indo-English Literature*. Jalandhar: ABS Publishers, 1994.

Barthes, Roland. *The Semiotic Challenge* (Translated by Richard Howard). New York: Blackwell, 1988.

Benson, Eugene. *Encyclopedia of Post-Colonial Literatures in English*. London: Routledge, 1994.

Bhabha, Homi K. *Locations of Culture: Discussing Postcolonial Culture*. London: Routledge, 1996.

——. *Nation and Narration*. New York: Routledge, 1990.

Bhalla, Amrita. *Shashi Deshpande*. New Delhi: Atlantic Publishers, 2010.

Bharat, Meenakshi, ed. *Desert in Bloom*. New Delhi: Pencraft International, 2004.

Bhargava, Rajul and Shubhshree, eds. *Of Narratives and Narrators*. New Delhi and Jaipur: Rawat Publications, 2004.

Bharucha, Nilufer E. "Inhabiting Enclosures and Creating Spaces: The Worlds of Women in Indian Literature in English". *Ariel*, Vol. 29 No. 1, January 1998.

Bharucha, Nilufer E. and Vilas Sarang, eds. *Indian English Fiction, 1980–1990: An Assessment*. New Delhi: B.R.Pub.Corporation, 1994.

Bharucha, Nilufer E. and Vrinda Nabar, eds. *Mapping Cultural Spaces: Post-Colonial Indian Literature in English*. New Delhi: Vision Books, 1998.

Booth, Wayne. *The Rhetoric of Fiction*. Chicago: University of Chicago Press, 1961.

Bose, Buddhadeva. *The Book of Yudhishthir: A Study of the Mahabharat of Vyas* (Translated by Sujit Mukherjee from Bengali).Orient Longman, 1986.

Boulton, Marjorie. *The Anatomy of the Novel*. London and Boston: Routledge & Kegan Paul, 1975.

Bryant, Sara Cone. *The Storytelling Handbook*, ed. Arunima Sehgal Mukherjee. Chandigarh: Unistar Book Pvt. Ltd., 2004.

Brydon, Diana and Helen Tifflin, eds. *Decolonising Fictions*. Sydney, Australia: Dangaroo, 1993.

Buck, William. *Ramayana* (Retold by William Buck). New York: A Mentor Book, 1976.

Burton, Antoinettee M. *Gender, Sexuality and Colonial Modernities*. London: Routledge, 1999.

Buscall, Jon and Outi Pickering, eds. *Approaches to Narrative Fiction*. Turku Fin: University of Turku, 1999.

Carr, E.H. *What is History*. New York: Knopf, 1961.

Chandgadkar, Swati. "A Not so Feministic Tale: Review of *A Matter of Time*". *Femina*, 1 April, 1997.

Chandra, Sudhir. *The Oppressive Present*. New Delhi: OUP, 1992.

——. *Continuing Dilemmas: Understanding Social Consciousness*. New Delhi: Tulika, 2002.

Chandra, Suresh. "Semiotics of Feminist Discourse in *That Long Silence*". *Critical Practice*, Vol. 3, No. 3, January 1996.

Chatterjee, Chandra. *The World Within: A Study of Novels in English by Indian Women*. New Delhi: Radha Publications, 1996.

Childs, Peter and Patrick Williams, eds. *Modernism: The New Critical Idiom*. London: Routledge, 2000.

Cramer, P. *Story Telling, Narrative and the Thematic Apperception Test*. New York: Guilford Press, 1996.

Culler, Jonathan. *Structuralist Poetics*. London: Routledge, 1975.

Daiches, David. *Critical Approaches to Novel*. London: Longman, 1964.

——. *The Novel and the Modern World*. Chicago and London: Chicago Press, 1965.

Das, Veena and R.K. Dhawan, eds. *Fiction of the Nineties*. New Delhi: Prestige, 1994.

Das, Veena. *Critical Events*. Delhi: Oxford University Press, 1995.

De Beauvoir, Simone. *The Second Sex*. Middlesex: Penguin Books, 1972.

Derrida, Jacques. "Structure, Sign and Play in the Discourse of Human Sciences" (Rpt in abbreviated form in K.M. Newton's *Twentieth Century Literary Theory: A Reader*) London: Macmillan, 1988.

Dhanju, Jaspal Kaur. *History and Postmodernism*. Chandigarh: Unistar, 2006.

Dharwadker, Vinay, ed. *The Collected Essays of A.K. Ramanujan*. New Delhi: OUP, 2004.

Dhawan, R.K., ed. *Comparative Literature*. New Delhi: Bahari Publications, 1987.

——. *Indian Women Novelists*. New Delhi: Prestige, 1991.

Donovan, Josephine, ed. *Feminist Literary Criticism: Explorations in Theory*. Kentucky: The University Press of Kentucky, 1998.

Dowson, Jane and Steven Earnshaw, eds. *Postmodern Subjects/Postmodern Texts*. Atlanta, GA: Rodopi, 1995.

Earnshaw, Steven. *Just Postmodernism*. Atlanta: Rodopi, 1997.

Edel, Leon, ed. *The Selected Letters of Henry James*. New York: Farrar, Straus & Cudahy, 1956.

Felman, Shoshana, ed. *Literature and Psychoanalysis*. London: John Hopkins University Press, 1982.

Felski, Rita. *Beyond Feminist Aesthetics: Feminist Literature and Social Change*. Cambridge: Harvard University Press, 1989.

Fillingham, Lydia A. *Foucault*. Chennai: Orient Longman, 2000.

Forster, E.M. *Aspects of the Novel*. Harmondsworth: Penguin, 1963.

Gadgil, Gangadhar. *Indian Literature: Issues and Explorations*. New Delhi: B.R. Publishing Corporation, 1995.

Ghadially, Rehana, ed. *Women in Indian Society: A Reader*. New Delhi: Sage, 1988.

Gupta, Santosh. "The Binding Vine of Relationships in Shashi Deshpande's Novels." *Critical Practice*, Vol. VI, No. 2, June 1998.

Handy, William J. and Max Westbrook, eds. *Twentieth Century Criticism*. New Delhi: Light and Life Publishers, 1974.

Hawkes, Terence. *Structuralism and Semiotics*. London: Methuen, 1977.

Heilburn, Carolyn G. *Writing and Woman's Life*. New York: Ballantine Books, 1998.

Hugh, Mercer Curtler. *Rediscovering Values: Coming to Terms with Postmodernism*. New York: Armonk, 1997.

Hutcheon, Linda. *A Poetics of Postmodernism: History, Theory, Fiction*. London and New york: Routledge, 1988.

——. *A Theory of Parody: The Teachings of Twentieth Century Art Forms*. Champaign and Urbana: University of Illinois Press, 2001.

Iyengar, K.R. Srinivasa. *Indian Writing in English*. New Delhi: Sterling Publishers, 1985.

Jackson, Rosemary. *Fantasy: The Literature of Subversion*. London: Methuen, 1981.

Jackson, Stevi and Jackie Jones. *Contemporary Feminist Theories*. New York: New York UP, 1998.

Jain, Jasbir and Avadhesh Singh, eds. *Indian Feminisms*. New Delhi: Creative Books, 2001.

Jain, Jasbir and Supriya Agarwal, eds. *Gender and Narrative*. Jaipur and New Delhi: Rawat Publications, 2002.

Jain, Jasbir and Veena Singh, eds. *Contesting Postcolonialisms*. Jaipur and New Delhi: Rawat Publications, 2004.

Jain, Jasbir. *Stairs to the Attic: The Novels of Anita Desai*. Jaipur: Printwell, 1987.

——. *Writing Women across Cultures*. Jaipur and New Delhi: Rawat Publications, 2002.

——. *Gendered Realities, Human Spaces: The Writing of Shashi Deshpande*. Jaipur and New Delhi: Rawat Publications, 2003.

——. "Shashi Deshpande". *A Companion to Indian Fiction in English*. Ed. Pier Piciucco. New Delhi: Atlantic Publishers, 2004.

——. *Beyond Postcolonialism: Dreams and Realities of a Nation*. Jaipur and New Delhi: Rawat Publications, 2006.

——, ed. *Creating Theory: Writers on Writing*. New Delhi: Pencraft International, 2000.

——, ed. *Women in Patriarchy*. Jaipur and New Delhi: Rawat Publications, 2005

——, ed. *Women's Writing: Text and Context*. Jaipur and New Delhi: Rawat Publications, 1996.

Jain, Naresh K., ed. *Women in Indo-Anglian Fiction: Tradition and Modernity*. New Delhi: Manohar, 1998.

James, Henry. *The House of Fiction*, ed. Leon Edel. London: Mercury Books, 1962.

Juneja, O.P. *Post Colonial Novel*. New Delhi: Creative Books, 1995.

Kakar, Sudhir. *Intimate Relations: Exploring Indian Sexuality*. New Delhi: Penguin, 1989.

——. *The Inner World: A Psycho-analytic Study of Childhood and Society in India*. New Delhi: OUP, 2002.

Karl, Frederic R. and Marvin Magalaner. *A Reader's Guide to Great Twentieth Century English Novels*. London: Thames and Hudson, 1961.

Karve, Iravati. *Yuganta: The End of an Epoch*. Mumbai: Orient Longman, 1994.

Katrak, Ketu H. "Decolonizing Culture: Toward a Theory for Postcolonial Women's Texts". *Modern Fiction Studies*, Vol. 28, No. 1, Winter 1989.

Kaufmall, Walter, ed. *Existentialism from Dostoevsky to Sartre*. New York: New American Library, 1975.

Kenon, Shlomith Rimmon. *Narrative Fiction: Contemporary Poetics*. London and New York: Routledge, 2002.

Kirpal, Viney and Mukta Atrey. *Shashi Deshpande: A Feminist Study of Her Fiction*. New Delhi: B.R. Publishing Corporation, 1998.

Kirpal, Viney. "What is the Modern Third World Novel". *Journal of Commonwealth Literature*, Vol. XXIII, No. 1, 1988.

——, ed. *The New Indian Novel in English*. Bombay: Allied Publishers Ltd., 1990.

——, ed. *The Postmodern Novel*. Mumbai: Allied Publishers, 1996.

Klooss, Wolfgang, ed. *Across the Lines: Intertextuality and Transcultural Communication in the New Literatures in English*. Amsterdam Rodopi, 1998.

Kroeber, Karl. *Retelling/Rereading: The Fate of Storytelling in Modern Times*. New Jersey: Rutgers University Press, 2001.

Lal, Lakshmi. *Myth and Me: The Indian History*. New Delhi: Roopa & Company, 2003.

Lenntrichia and Thomas Laughlin, eds. *Critical Terms for Literary Study*. Chicago: University of Chicago Press, 1995.

Lerner, Laurence. *The Frontiers of Literature*. Oxford: Basil Blackwell, 1988.

Levi-Strauss, Claude. *The Savage Mind*. London: Weidenfeld & Nicolson, 1996.

Lodge, David, ed. *Twentieth Century Literary Criticism*. London: Longman, 1972.

Malinowski, Bronislaw. *Myth in Primitive Psychology* (Rpt., Originally published in 1927). London: Routledge, 2002.

McNay, Lois. *Foucault: A Critical Introduction*. New York: Continnum, 1994.

Menturn, Leigh. *Sita's Daughters: Coming Out of Purdah*. New York: Oxford University Press, 1993.

Miller, J.H., ed. *Aspects of Narrative*. New York: Columbia University Press, 1971.

Morris, Pam, *Realism: The New Critical Idiom Series*. London: Routledge, 2003.

Mukherjee, Meenakshi, ed. *Rushdie's Midnight's Children: A Book of Readings*. Delhi: Pencraft International, 2003.

——. *Realism and Reality: The Novel and Society in India*. Delhi: OUP, 1985.

——. *Twice Born Fiction: Themes and Techniques of the Indian Novel in English*. New Delhi: Pencraft International, 2001.

Naik, Chanchala K., ed. *Writing Difference: The Novels of Shashi Deshpande*. New Delhi: Pencraft International, 2005.

Naik, M.K. *Twentieth Century Indian English Fiction*. New Delhi: Pencraft International, 2004.

Naik, M.K. and Shyamala A. Narayan. *Indian English Literature: A Critical Survey*. New Delhi: Pencraft International, 2004.

Nair, Rukmini Bhaya. *Narrative Gravity: Conversation, Cognition, Culture*. New Delhi: OUP, 2002.

Nandy, Ashis. *The Intimate Enemy: Loss and Recovery of the Self under Colonialism*. Delhi: Oxford University Press, 1988.

Naravene, V.S. *Best Stories from the Indian Classics* (Selected and Retold by Naravene). New Delhi: Roli Books, 1994.

Narayan, Uma. *Dislocating Cultures, Identities, Traditions and Third World Feminism*. New York: Routledge, 1997.

Neisser, Ulric and Robyn Fivush, eds. *The Remembering Self: Construction and Accuracy in the Self-Narrative*. Cambridge: Cambridge University Press, 1994.

Nichol, Bran, ed. *Postmodernism and the Contemporary Fiction*. Edinburgh: Edinburgh University Press, 2002.

Nicholas, Zurbrugg. *The Parameters of Post-Modernism*. Carbondale: Southern Illinois University Press, 1993.

Norris, Christopher. *Deconstruction: Theory and Practice*. London: Routledge, 1991.

O' Flahetty, Wendy Doniger. *Hindu Myths*. Harmondsworth: Penguin, 1978.

O'Donnell, Kevin. *Postmodernism*. London: Lion Publishing Plc., 2003.

Ong, Walter J. *Orality and Literacy: The Technologising of the Word*. London: Methuen, 1982.

Palmer, Pauline. *Contemporary Women's Fiction: Narrative Practices and Feminist Practices*. New York: Harvester Wheatsheaf, 1989.

Pandey, Suryanath, ed. *Contemporary Indian Women Writers in English*. New Delhi: Atlantic Publishers, 1999.

Pathak, R.S., ed. *The Fiction of Shashi Deshpande.* New Delhi: Creative Books, 1998.

——, ed. *Recent Indian Fiction.* New Delhi: Prestige Books, 1994.

——. *Modern Indian Novel in English.* New Delhi: Creative Books, 1999.

Price, Reynolds. *A Palpable God: Thirty Stories Translated from the Bible.* New York: Atheneum,1978.

Rabkin, Eric S. *The Fantastic in Literature.* New Jersey: Princeton University Press,1976.

Raisinghani, Neelam, ed. *Realism, Reality and Fiction: Essays on the Indian Novels.* Jaipur: Best Book Company, 2006.

Rajan, Gita and Radhika Mohanram, eds. *Postcolonial Discourse and Changing Cultural Context: Theory and Criticism.* Westport: Greenwood Press, 1996.

Rajan, Gita. *Real and Imagined Women: Gender, Culture and Postcolonialism.* London: Routledge, 1993.

Rajan, Rajeshwari Sunder. "The Feminist Plot and the Nationalist Allegory: Home and World in Two Indian Women's Novels in English". *Modern Fiction Studies,* Vol. 39, No. 1, Winter, 1993.

Rao, A.C., ed. *Myth and History in Contemporary Indian Novel in English.* New Delhi: Atlantic Publishers and Distributors, 2005.

Rao, Vimala C. "History as Metafiction: The Ayodhya Theme: A Reading of Shashi Deshpande's *Small Remedies.*" *Littcrit* 54, Vol. 28, No. 2, December 2002.

Ray, Mohit K. and Rama Kundu, eds. *Studies in Women Writers in English,* Vol. 3. New Delhi: Atlantic Publishers & Distributors, 2005.

Rice, Philip and Patricia Waugh, eds. *Modern Literary Theory: A Reader.* London: Arnold, 2001.

Roberts, Andrew Michael, ed. *The Novel from its Origin to the Present Day.* London: Bloomsbury, 1994.

Roberts, Geoffrey, ed. *The History and Narrative Reader.* London & New York: Routledge, 2001.

Roy, Anuradha. *Patterns of Feminist Consciousness in Indian Women Writers.* New Delhi: Prestige Books,1991.

Rushdie, Salman. *Haroun and the Sea of Stories*. London: Granta Books, 1990.

——. "Midnight's Children and Shame." *Kunapipi* VII, 1, 1985.

——. "Midnight's Children and Shame." *Kunapipi* IV, 2, 1982.

——. *Midnight's Children*. London: Jonathan Cape, 1981.

San Juan, Epifanio. *Hegemonies and Strategies of Transgression*. Albany, New York: State University of New York, 1995.

Sandhu, Sarabjit. *The Image of Woman in the Novels of Shashi Deshpande*. New Delhi: Prestige, 1991.

Satchidanandan, K. *Author, Text, Issues: Essays on Indian Literature*. New Delhi: Pencraft International, 2003.

Scholes, Robert and Robert Kellogg. *The Nature of Narrative*. New York: Oxford University Press, 1966.

Sebastian, Mrinalini. *The Enterprise of Reading Differently: The Novels of Shashi Deshpande in Postcolonial Arguments*. New Delhi: Prestige, 2000.

Sharma, K.K. *Modern Fictional Theorists*. Delhi: Vimal Prakashan, 1981.

Shastri, Sudha. *Intertextuality and Victorian Studies*. Hyderabad: Orient Longman, 2001.

Shirwadakar, Meena. *Image of Women in Indo-Anglian Novel*. New Delhi: Sterling, 1979.

Singer, Jerome L. *Day Dreaming and Fantasy*. London: George Allen and Unwin Ltd., 1975.

Singh, Khushwant and Shobha De, eds. *Uncertain Laisons*. New Delhi: Penguin India,1993.

Singh, Sushila. *Feminism and Recent Fiction in English*. New Delhi: Prestige,1991.

——. *Feminism: Theory, Criticism, Analysis*. New Delhi: Pencraft International, 1997.

Slemon, Stephen. "Post-Colonial Allegory and the Transformation of History". *Journal of Commonwealth Literature*, Vol. 23, No. 1, 1988.

Soyinka, Wole. *Myth, Literature and the African World*. Cambridge, UK: Cambridge UP, 1990.

Srivastava, Sharad. *The New Women in Indian English Fiction*. New Delhi: Creative Books, 1996.

Tharoor, Shashi. *The Great Indian Novel*. New Delhi: Penguin, 1989.

Tharu, Susie and K. Lalita, eds. *Women Writing in India 600 B.C. to the Present*. Delhi: OUP, 1991.

Todorov, Tzvetan. *The Poetics of Prose* (Originally published in French, 1971). Oxford: Blackwell, 1977.

Trivedi, Harish and Meenakshi Mukherjee, eds. *Interrogating Post-Colonialism: Theory, Text and Context*. Shimla: Indian Institute of Advanced Study, 1996.

Vantier, Marie. *New World Myth: Postmodernism and Postcolonialism*. Montreal: McGill Queen's UP, 1998.

Walder, Dennis. *Post-Colonial Literatures in English History: Language, Theory*. Oxford: Blackwell, 1998.

Walker, Nancy A. *Feminist Alternatives: Irony and Fantasy in the Contemporary Novels by Women*. Jackson: University Press of Mississippi, 1990.

Watt, Ian. *The Rise of the Novel*. Berkeley: University of California Press, 1959.

Waugh, Patricia, ed. *Literary Theory and Criticism: An Oxford Guide*. Delhi: OUP, 2006.

——, ed. *Postmodernism: A Reader*. London: Arnold, 1992.

Woolf, Leonard, ed. *A Writer's Diary*. London: The Hogarth Press, 1953.

Woolf, Virginia. *A Room of One's Own*. London: Grafton Books, 1989.

Wright, Elizabeth. *Psychoanalytic Criticism: Theory in Practice*. London: Methuen, 1984.

Index